SIMPLE DBT COPING SKILLS

SIMPLE DBT COPING SKILLS

75 Ways to Live Mindfully, Regulate Emotions, Manage Distress, and Improve Relationships

SUZETTE BRAY, LMFT

Cover Designer: Will Mack
Interior Designer: Joshua R. Moore
Illustrations by Shutterstock: © Rakib188: cover, throughout (botanical shapes); © FishCoolish: 7, 121 (high five); © Lokman_Shekh: 22; © Jeremy Show: 23, 32, 97; © Karim Osama: 44; © papa papong: 52; © saepul_bahri: 67
Getty Images: © Dmytro Lukyanets/iStock: 5, 133 (scale); © Lentochka/iStock: 5, 133 (heart); © koxeiryu/iStock: 5 (arrows); © Sudowoodo/iStock: 7, 17, 85, 106, 117 (heads & clouds), 20; © YoGinta/iStock: 7, 49, 81 (happy & sad faces); © Rudzhan Nagiev/iStock: 24; © bsd studio/iStock: 34, 42, 85 (person & heart); © Coquet Adrien/iStock: 37 (smiley face); © texturis/iStock: 49 (heart hands); © Muhammad Shabraiz/iStock: 49 (person & faces); © gentle studio/iStock: 72; © Panyapat Pikunkaew/iStock: 92; © azzurri/Digital Vision Vectors: 112 (case); © eyewave/iStock: 112 (gum); © Abbasy Kautsar/iStock: 112 (hand sanitizer); © yugoro/iStock: 112 (phone); © Giorgi Gogitidze/iStock: 212 (hand, people & heart)
© Sean Sims: 41
© Conor Buckley: 53
© Christy Ni: 105
Author photo courtesy of Linda Bradley Photography
Art Director: Lisa Schreiber
Art Producer: Stacey Stambaugh
Editor: Adrian Potts
Production Editor: Rachel Taenzler
Production Designer: Jeffrey Piekarz

Published by Callisto Publishing LLC C/O Sourcebooks LLC
P.O. Box 4410, Naperville, Illinois 60567-4410
(630) 961-3900
callistopublishing.com

Library of Congress Cataloging-in-Publication Data is on file with the publisher.

Printed and bound in China.
OGP 10 9 8 7 6 5 4 3 2 1

CONTENTS

INTRODUCTION

Welcome to DBT. This book is filled with coping skills from dialectical behavior therapy, more commonly known as DBT. This is the resource I wish I had when I was first learning DBT many years ago, the one I could easily hand to my clients and others I teach about DBT. Think of it as a tool kit for living fully in the moment, managing big emotions, coping with distress, and improving your relationships. Don't worry if you're new to DBT. This book is designed to be accessible whether you've never heard of DBT or are already familiar with it.

In my more than twenty-five years as a marriage and family therapist—owning and operating a comprehensive DBT program for many years, and now in private practice offering DBT-informed therapy—I've seen again and again how life-changing these skills can be.

I use these skills daily as a therapist, business owner, mom, and, most importantly, human being. Like so many people, I wasn't taught these skills growing up. Learning them was transformational, and I'm thrilled to share them with you now.

I liken DBT skills to a new language that you will learn to speak fluently. Some parts will feel natural and stick right away, while others will take more time and practice to master. But don't worry; you've got your DBT dictionary (this book) to help you.

This is a user-friendly guide to learning and using daily DBT coping skills to manage challenging emotions and stressful situations. These coping skills are mental and emotional first aid strategies: actions you take to calm down and make wise choices even when things feel overwhelming.

Whether you're in therapy or learning these skills alone, by the end of this book, you'll have a handy set of tools to help you move through life with more ease, more control over your emotions, and greater effectiveness in your relationships.

HOW TO USE THIS BOOK

One of the biggest challenges of being a DBT therapist is that teaching a comprehensive DBT program to patients takes about six months. Knowing that these tools can help when someone is struggling is frustrating, but it takes time to teach everything immediately.

This book is a game changer for you, because it provides:

- A simple introduction to DBT basics.
- Seventy-five DBT tools that are right at your fingertips whenever you need them. Plus, cheat sheets at the start of each section and trackers at the end to make learning as easy as possible.
- Space to customize your very own DBT Tool Kit (pages 148–149) of the skills you find are most useful in everyday life, so that you can be prepared for any situation.

There's no right or wrong way to use this book. When you need a skill, you can flip to the section that's most relevant to what you're dealing with. However, I encourage you to read the whole book to get a good overview of all the available tools.

Section 1 of the book contains a primer on DBT and its uses. Sections 2 to 5 are grouped according to DBT's four areas, or "modules."

DBT MODULE	BOOK SECTION
Mindfulness	➔ Skills to Live in the Moment (page 15)
Emotional Regulation	➔ Skills to Handle Big Emotions (page 47)
Distress Tolerance	➔ Skills to Cope with Distress (page 83)
Interpersonal Effectiveness	➔ Skills for Better Relationships (page 119)

Each section provides examples of how to use the skills, a cheat sheet to guide you, and a skills tracker at the end. Tracking isn't just a way to measure progress; it helps you build better habits. Plus, it will show you which skills work best when life gets messy.

With consistency and practice, you will notice the work getting easier. Even small changes add up over time, making a big difference in handling emotions, relationships, and life's challenges.

I'm so excited to be on this journey with you. Let's get started!

SECTION 1

The Basics of DBT

Welcome to the basics of dialectical behavior therapy, more commonly known as DBT. Unlike some forms of therapy that focus on changing thoughts or gaining insight, DBT gives you strategies you can use in the moment when emotions threaten to derail you. This section sets you up for success as you move through the rest of the book. Here, you'll learn:

- What DBT is and how it developed.
- Who benefits from DBT (spoiler: everyone!).
- How DBT skills work and why they're so effective.
- The balance of acceptance and change (a core DBT concept).
- The four areas of DBT skills and how they fit together.
- By the end, you'll clearly understand how DBT skills can help you build a life that feels more balanced, fulfilling, and in control.

What Is DBT?

The cool thing about DBT is that, unlike more traditional therapies, it doesn't just focus on changing how you think, processing how you feel, or gaining insight. DBT goes beyond these essential skills and teaches you precisely what to do when emotions are overwhelming.

When emotions run high, it's hard to think clearly, let alone devise a plan to reason. DBT is like having a recipe for your emotions. It provides clear steps to follow when your emotions heat up, making you less likely to create a mess. That's part of why the psychologist Dr. Marsha Linehan developed DBT in the 1980s. She noticed that many of her patients struggled with emotions so intense that their attempts to cope often made things worse. Dr. Linehan discovered that linking cognitive behavioral therapy (CBT), which focuses on change, with Eastern mindfulness practices, which emphasize acceptance, was the right combination. Pairing these two practices helps people learn how to ride out challenging emotions.

So often, people see negative emotions as something to escape from as quickly as possible, particularly feelings of distress. DBT is nonjudgmental; emotions are neither "good" nor "bad." The practice teaches you to view emotions as signals that help you understand what is happening and how your reactions impact you. It is essential to realize that the goal of DBT isn't necessarily to feel better (though that can often happen!) but to get better at feeling your emotions and pushing disruptive emotions to the curb when they arise. When emotions aren't running the show, they stop becoming barriers to your goals.

WHO BENEFITS FROM DBT?

In the DBT world, we use the phrase "emotional dysregulation" a lot. Let's unpack that term so you'll understand what it means. For some people, emotions can feel like tidal waves; they hit fast and hard and seem impossible to control. When these emotional waves crash, focusing on what serves your short-term or long-term goals can be challenging. DBT is about learning to ride those waves instead of drowning in them.

Here's the thing: Emotional dysregulation affects everyone, though it manifests differently for each person. Some individuals experience it daily, while others feel it less frequently. For many, much depends on their stress levels, circumstances, or emotional triggers (like a stressful event). That's why DBT is so helpful.

When I introduce DBT skills to people in treatment, their loved ones, or even folks who aren't in therapy, I often hear the same response: "Why didn't I learn this as a kid? Life would have been so much easier!" Thankfully, DBT skills are starting to be taught in some schools, but the great news is that these skills can be learned by anyone at any time.

Dr. Linehan initially developed DBT for individuals struggling with borderline personality disorder symptoms like chronic suicidality and self-harm. But clinicians quickly saw its broader potential. Research has since shown DBT's effectiveness for people dealing with:

- Depression and anxiety
- Bipolar disorder
- Eating disorders
- Substance abuse
- PTSD and trauma

DBT can help anyone who needs support in dealing with their emotions. DBT offers tools to help you cope with whatever life throws your way in a way that leads to relief, not regret.

HOW DO DBT COPING SKILLS HELP?

When emotions take over, we can often act in ways that don't align with our values and don't help us reach our goals. You may even end up making a situation worse. DBT coping skills help you respond in ways that support what you truly want, not just what your momentary urges tell you to do. DBT skills teach you how to cope with distress in healthy ways and build stronger, more meaningful relationships. The coping tools can help with everyday challenges such as:

- **Acting without thinking:** Strong emotions can tempt us to say or do things we regret later, like lashing out in anger, making harmful decisions, or doing things that can damage relationships.

- **Avoiding problems:** Sometimes we fear strong emotions so much that we avoid situations altogether. Maybe you've ghosted someone instead of having a tough conversation or procrastinated on a task because you're afraid of failing or feeling incompetent.
- **Feeling overwhelmed:** When emotions hit like a tidal wave, it's easy to feel overcome entirely by rage, uncontrollable tears, or anxiety attacks.

With these tools, you don't have to be at the mercy of your emotions. You can learn to work *with* them, manage them effectively, feel them when necessary, and step away when it's wise.

The Roles of Acceptance and Change in DBT

DBT's approach to managing emotions is built on helping you cultivate a balance of acceptance and change.

- **Acceptance** is about seeing reality clearly, without judgment. It helps you stop wasting energy fighting situations that are outside your control.
- **Change** is about taking action, responding to emotions more effectively, and moving toward your goals.

These two ideas may seem like opposites, but they can both be true simultaneously. It's like saying, "I'm doing the best I can right now, and I can still work toward something better." Knowing when to lean on acceptance strategies and when to focus on change strategies is key to managing emotions and building the life each of us wants.

This balance of opposing truths is a method of engagement referred to as "dialectics." Dialectal thinking helps you embrace a middle path, steering clear of all-or-nothing or black-and-white thinking that can keep you stuck in intense emotions or create conflict in your relationships.

Finding Wisdom in Opposites!

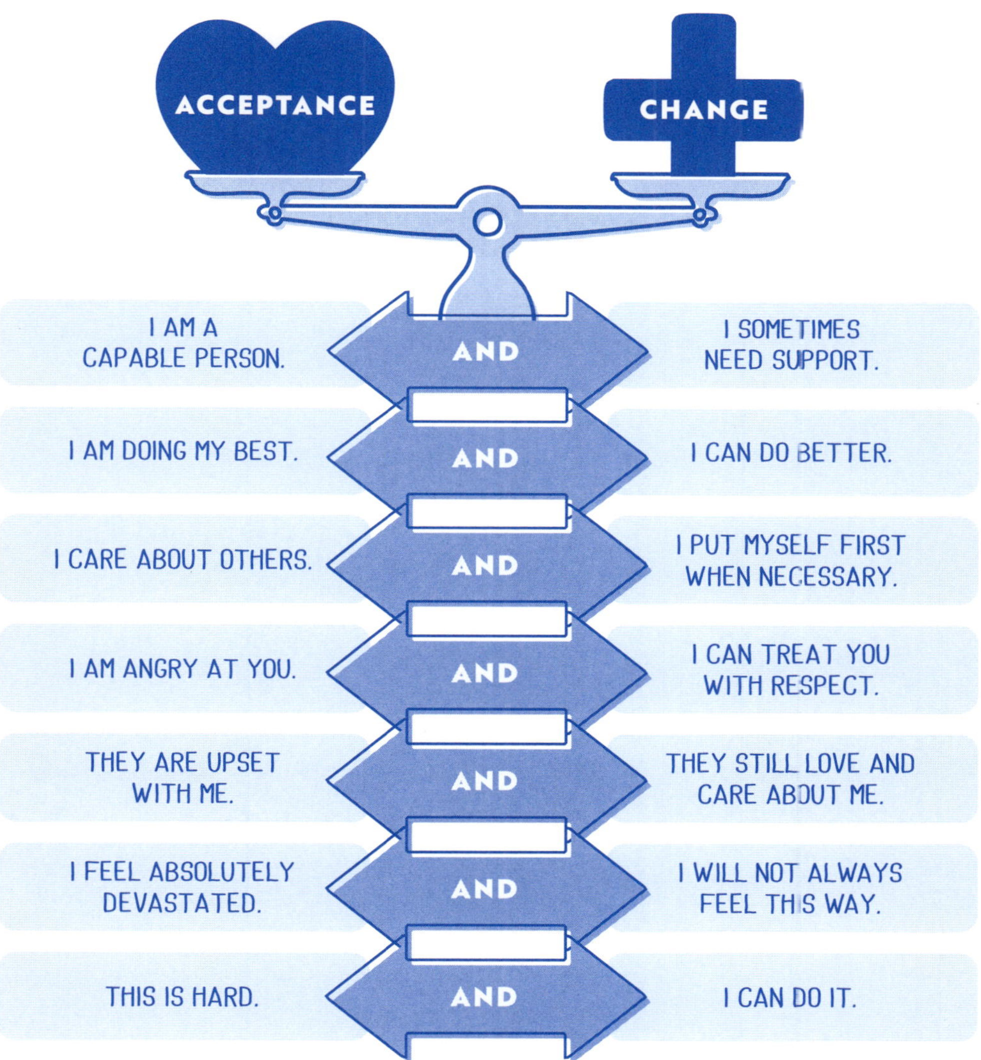

By embracing dialectical thinking, you can stay flexible and balanced and navigate life's challenges with clarity and compassion.

The Four Areas of DBT Skills

DBT skills are divided into four modules. The structure reflects the dialectical theme. The first two modules—Mindfulness and Distress Tolerance—focus on acceptance, while the remaining two—Emotional Regulation and Interpersonal Effectiveness—focus on change.

1. **Mindfulness:** This is about being fully present in the moment without judgment. It involves observing and describing reality rather than getting caught up in assumptions or judgments. These skills are foundational and can be found in page 15 in the Skills to Live in the Moment section.

2. **Distress Tolerance:** This has two main components. The first is a set of crisis survival skills, which help you get through challenging situations without making things worse. The second is radical acceptance, which enables you to accept the things you cannot change, whether in the moment or over the long term. These skills are covered in Skills to Cope with Distress, beginning on page 83.

3. **Emotional Regulation:** This module is about identifying emotions, evaluating whether the situation justifies them, and deciding how to respond. You'll learn when to change the emotion and when to process it by feeling it fully and then moving on. These skills are detailed in the Skills to Handle Big Emotions section, starting on page 47.

4. **Interpersonal Effectiveness:** These skills help you make it more likely to get what you need while maintaining your relationships and self-respect. To dive deeper into these tools, turn to Skills for Better Relationships, beginning on page 119.

Acceptance | **Change**

MINDFULNESS

Being present and accepting the current moment without judgment

EMOTIONAL REGULATION

Handling intense emotions so that you are less vulnerable to them

DISTRESS TOLERANCE

Managing a crisis without making the situation worse and accepting reality as it is

INTERPERSONAL EFFECTIVENESS

Getting your needs met and building healthy relationships

Make Friends with Your Parts

Do you ever feel like different parts of you are battling against one another? Like a tug-of-war is going on inside your mind? Maybe one part of you wants to avoid a difficult situation, while another feels guilty for not handling it immediately. This is a common experience.

Sometimes, we learn these responses early in life, usually to protect ourselves. For example, shutting down may have been a way to survive overwhelming chaos in childhood. The same goes for getting angry quickly; it may have helped you feel in control when you felt powerless. At the time, these responses helped you cope with what you were facing. But now, they likely do more harm than good.

The good news is you no longer need to fight these parts of yourself. This book will teach you how to make friends with them. Imagine these parts as younger versions of you, still protecting you the only way they know how. By approaching them with curiosity and kindness, you can start to understand what they're trying to do for you. Ask yourself: What is this part of me trying to accomplish? What need or fear is it responding to?

When you approach your emotions with compassion, you can find new ways to meet those needs without self-criticism or shame. Rather than being at war with yourself, you can create a sense of balance and teamwork within. Every part of you is doing its best; you can take the lead and guide them in a healthier direction.

That's where DBT skills come in. They teach you new and more effective ways to respond to challenges. As you make friends with all of your parts, you can gently guide them away from old reactive habits and toward more skillful responses that truly support your well-being.

Identify Your DBT Goals

The great thing about DBT skills is that they can be tailored to your specific needs. Take a moment to reflect on what you'd like to gain from learning these skills. Check off any of these common goals that resonate with you, and feel free to add your own.

- Respond to anger more calmly.
- Stop shutting people out when upset.
- Cope with anxiety without avoiding anxiety-provoking situations.
- Feel less overwhelmed by emotions.
- Improve communication with loved ones.
- Set and maintain boundaries with others.
- Handle difficult conversations without being defensive.
- Accept things I cannot change instead of fighting reality.
- Deal with fears of abandonment in ways that don't ultimately push people away (like blowing up someone's phone with too many texts or making threats).
- Build resilience so I don't feel as emotionally drained.
- Do what I need to do even if I don't feel like it.
- Cope with self-destructive urges in a healthy way.
- Stay present instead of getting lost in worries about the past or the future.
- Learn to validate myself instead of seeking outside approval.

MY PERSONAL DBT GOALS:

____

____

____

____

Whatever your goals are, the skills in this book will help you move toward them, one step at a time.

Choosing a DBT Skill to Use

The following table pairs DBT skills with common emotional struggles. All of these skills will be reviewed and explained in detail throughout the book. Remember, there are often multiple ways to respond skillfully when faced with a difficult situation. Some skills will feel like a perfect fit right away, while others may take practice. If a skill doesn't seem to help at first, don't give up! Try it again, tweak how you use it, or experiment with a different skill. Track what you try at the end of each section to see what works best for you.

IF YOU FEEL LIKE...	...THIS SKILL MIGHT HELP
I feel anxious, like something bad could happen.	**Check the Facts** (page 58)—look for actual evidence instead of assuming the worst.
I feel really angry at someone and want to lash out at them.	**STOP to Create Space** (page 89)—pause, take a step back, observe your urges, and proceed mindfully.
I'm worried that someone I love is going to turn against me and abandon me.	**Self-Soothe with Your Senses** (page 97)—engage in comforting activities that ground you in the present moment.
I want to stay in bed all day and avoid people, even though I have important things to do.	**Take Opposite Action** (page 60)—do the opposite of what your emotion tells you to do.
My heart is racing, and I think I might have a panic attack.	**TIPP with Paced Breathing** (page 94) and **TIPP with Paired Muscle Relaxation** (page 95)—slow your breathing and relax your muscles to signal safety to your body.

IF YOU FEEL LIKE...	...THIS SKILL MIGHT HELP
I feel like I am a terrible person.	**Replace Judgment with Facts** (page 30)—replace harsh self-judgment with objective facts.
I have the urge to do something self-destructive.	**Pros and Cons of Crisis Urges** (page 90)—consider the short-term and long-term consequences of engaging in the urge.
I feel really worn down and more emotional than usual.	**PLEASE to Manage Emotions** (page 71)—take care of your body to reduce vulnerability to negative emotions.
I can't stop worrying about a mistake I made.	**Wise Mind ACCEPTS** (page 96)—distract yourself from worries that you cannot do anything about.
I can't fall asleep.	**Improve Your Sleep Hygiene** (page 72)—set up a consistent bedtime routine to signal to your body that it is time to rest.
I want to say no to something a person has asked me to do, but I'm scared to stand up for myself.	**DEAR MAN** (page 124), **GIVE** (page 125), **FAST** (page 126)—create a script to guide you in saying no while maintaining the relationship.
I feel really sad.	**Self-Validate to Honor Your Own Feelings** (page 136)—acknowledge your emotion as valid without judging yourself for feeling it.

Experiment with different skills, track your progress, and build your personal DBT tool kit, page 148. With time and practice, these skills will become second nature!

Tips for Using DBT Skills

DBT skills are powerful, but like any new tool, they can take time to master. I've seen patients practice a new skill for several weeks until they build a solid "muscle memory" and make it part of their repertoire. Here are some tips to help you get the most out of this book and your DBT journey:

- **Keep an Open Mind.** Some skills might feel awkward or unfamiliar at first. That's okay! The more you practice, the more natural they'll become. Give each skill at least a few chances before deciding that it is not for you.
- **Find What Works Best for You.** Not every skill will be your go-to. Experiment with different techniques three to five times to see what fits your personality, needs, and struggles. Over time, you'll build a personalized tool kit of skills that work for you.
- **Practice, Practice, Practice (and Practice Some More!).** One of the biggest mistakes people make is waiting to be in a crisis to use skills. I don't encourage you to do that. Instead, think of a situation where a skill might help, and then practice. Some skills only take five or ten minutes to practice, while others may take longer. The important thing is to keep practicing regularly, even in small doses, so when you need a skill, you're ready to go.
- **Consider DBT-Focused Therapy or Self-Help Options.** If you find the skills in this book helpful but want more guidance, consider enrolling in a comprehensive DBT program, working with a DBT-informed therapist, or joining a skills group. Check the Resources section (page 152) for information on finding support.
- **Create a Crisis Plan.** A premade crisis plan can guide you through intense moments safely, without reacting impulsively or making choices you might regret. There is space to create your own on page 150.

With time and consistency, these skills will become second nature. It will become easier to be skillful at managing your emotions and choosing effective behaviors. You are on your way!

SECTION 2

Skills to Live in the Moment

In this section, you'll learn the first skill set of DBT: mindfulness. Essentially, mindfulness means paying attention to the present moment without judgment and without trying to change it. In DBT, mindfulness is vital to recognizing the right skill for the situation. I introduce key DBT terms, including Wise Mind, Reasonable Mind, and Emotion Mind. Additionally, you'll complete several exercises that explain and explore the physical (the "What") and the cognitive (the "How") aspects of meditation.

Through mindfulness, you can become more cognizant of your thoughts, emotions, and urges and determine if your actions fit the situation and align with your long-term goals. When you're mindful, you can manage emotions more effectively, make better decisions, and ease stress. It's best to try the easier skills when you're in distress and the harder ones when you're calm.

Goals of Mindfulness

Mindfulness helps you access the wisest part of your mind to help make the best possible choices in any situation. The goals of mindfulness in DBT are to:

- ✓ **Access your inner wisdom:** Strengthen your ability to balance emotions and logic to make better decisions.
- ✓ **Increase awareness:** Notice thoughts, emotions, and surroundings instead of reacting on autopilot.
- ✓ **Boost focus and presence:** Improve concentration and fully engage in the present moment.
- ✓ **Manage emotions:** Prevent emotions from spiraling out of control by observing them without being overwhelmed.
- ✓ **Pause before reacting:** Create space between something that triggers a strong emotion and your reaction to it.
- ✓ **Let go of judgment:** See reality as it is rather than judging it as "good" or "bad."

When you practice mindfulness on a regular basis, it helps you develop greater control over your emotions and actions and find greater clarity when making decisions.

MINDFULNESS CHEAT SHEET

Skills to Live in the Moment

THREE STATES OF MIND

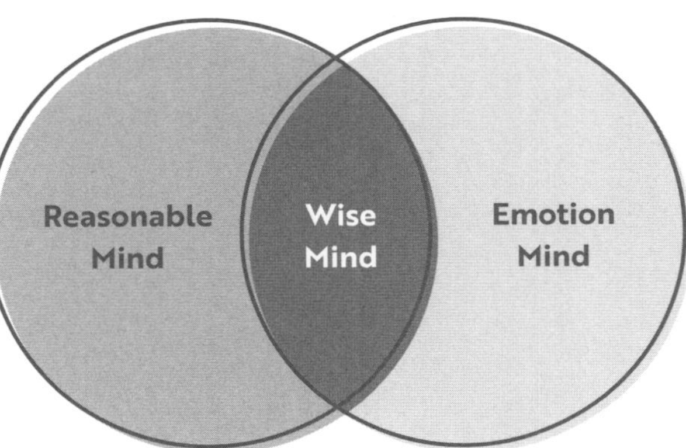

Reasonable Mind: Facts, logic, problem-solving

Wise Mind: Inner wisdom. Balances reason and emotion

Emotion Mind: Feelings, impulses, urges

THE "WHAT" SKILLS

What You Do When Being Mindful

- Leaves on a Stream
- 5-4-3-2-1 Grounding
- Urge Surfing
- Describe an Object with Facts
- Label Thoughts as Just Thoughts
- Participate Fully in the Moment

THE "HOW" SKILLS

How You Practice Mindfulness

- Replace Judgment with Facts
- Put Yourself in Their Shoes
- The One-Task Challenge
- Mindful Eating
- Move from "Right" to Effective
- Loving-Kindness Meditation

Bonus Mindfulness Skills

- Five-Finger Breathing
- Speak to Yourself with Compassion
- Accept Pleasant and Unpleasant Moments
- One Minute of Focus

Meet Your Wise Mind

- **Wise Mind:** This is the state that balances reason and emotion while adding intuition and deeper wisdom. It helps you make effective choices that honor your emotions and long-term goals. To get here, we must first discuss the two states of your Wise Mind that influence how you think and act: Reasonable Mind and Emotion Mind.
- **Reasonable Mind:** This part focuses on facts, logic, and problem-solving. It's great for making plans, analyzing situations, and completing tasks, but it can lead you to make decisions based on rules without considering your values or other factors.
- **Emotion Mind:** Feelings, impulses, and urges rule here. The mind reacts based on how you feel in the moment, often without considering long-term consequences. For example, if you feel fear (even if it isn't based on facts), you may avoid something important despite knowing it could benefit you.

The goal in DBT is to bring the Reasonable Mind and the Emotion Mind into harmony in the Wise Mind. To access Wise Mind, you must pause, check in with yourself, and consider reason and emotions before deciding. With practice, tuning into Wise Mind helps you respond thoughtfully rather than react impulsively. This allows you to regulate your emotions more skillfully and make better decisions.

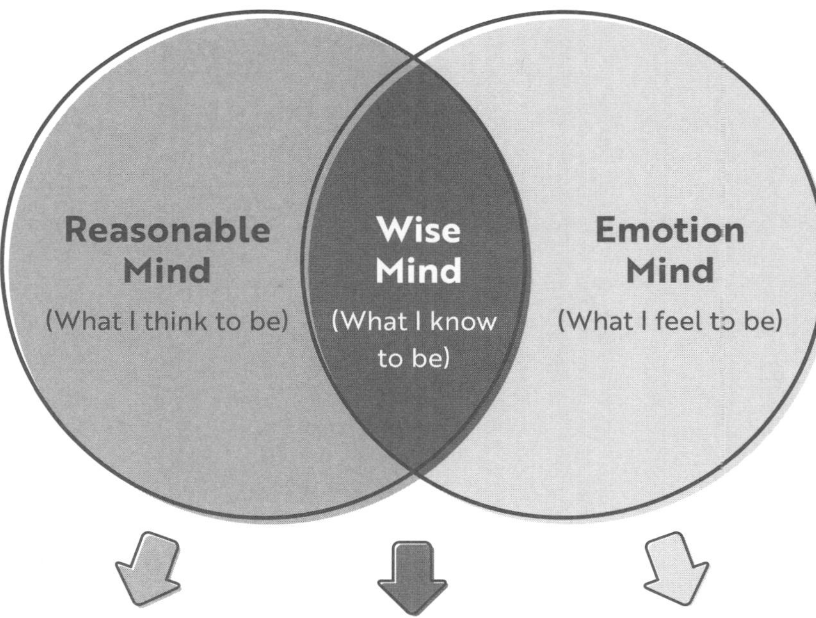

Ruled by logic, facts, and analysis, with little regard for emotions or personal values. Just the facts and only the facts.

Balances logic and emotion, considers values, and sees what truly matters. The inner wisdom within all of us that guides our best decisions.

Ruled by emotions and impulses, with no thought for consequences. "Make it stop!" or "I want more!"

SKILL 1

Wise Mind Breathing

This exercise calms your nervous system by slowing down your breath, making it easier to access your inner wisdom. Practice it regularly so you can readily reach this wisdom when overwhelmed by big emotions.

1. **Find a comfortable position:** Sit or stand in a relaxed posture. Close your eyes or softly focus on a spot in front of you.
2. **Take a deep breath in:** As you inhale, silently say to yourself, "Wise." Feel the air filling your lungs and your body expanding.
3. **Slowly exhale:** As you exhale, silently say, "Mind." Let go of tension and allow your body to relax.
4. **Repeat for a few rounds:** Continue breathing in "Wise" and out "Mind," letting each breath center you in the present moment.
5. **Notice the shift:** As you practice, check in with yourself. Do you feel more balanced? Remember, Wise Mind is always within you. Simply pause and listen.

When to use it? If you feel carried away by a strong emotion or feel the urge to act impulsively without thinking.

The "What" Skills of Mindfulness

These "What" exercises are designed to help you slow down and respond instead of reacting. Observing allows you to step back, Describing enables you to label what's happening, and Participating lets you engage fully in the present moment instead of getting stuck in your head. You can achieve "being present" when practicing mindfulness by employing these three skills.

- **Observe:** Use your senses to pay attention to your thoughts, feelings, and what's happening around you, without judging or labeling your experience.
- **Describe:** Put words to what you observe using facts, not opinions or assumptions. Remember, you can describe your own internal experience but can't know another person's internal experience.
- **Participate:** Engage fully in the present moment without distraction. The idea is to throw yourself entirely into the now.

SKILL 2

Leaves on a Stream

This observing skill teaches you to visualize your feelings as leaves gently floating down a stream. This practice allows your thoughts to come and go without you getting caught up or carried away by them.

1. **Bring awareness to the present moment:** Take a few slow, deep breaths. Notice the sensation of air entering and leaving your body. Feel your feet on the ground and your hands resting in your lap.
2. **Picture a gentle stream:** Imagine yourself sitting beside a slow-moving stream. The water flows steadily, carrying leaves along its surface. Each leaf moves at its own pace, some drifting quickly, others slowly.
3. **Place your thoughts or feelings on the leaves:** As a thought or feeling arises, notice it without judgment. Instead of engaging with it, place it on a leaf and watch it float downstream.
4. **Keep watching without controlling:** Let the leaves come and go naturally. If one gets stuck, gently remind yourself that thoughts and emotions pass independently like the leaves. If you get distracted, return to the stream and continue observing.
5. **Return to the present moment:** After a few minutes, bring your attention back to your breath. Notice how you feel without judging the experience. Open your eyes and take a deep breath before moving on with your day.

When to use it? When you are hung up on an idea or feeling you can't get out of your mind.

5-4-3-2-1 Grounding

This simple countdown helps you refocus by engaging your senses. It shifts your attention away from thoughts and worries to the present moment, as you observe small sensory details that you might usually tune out.

5 Things You Can See

Look around and name (either out loud or in your head) five things you can see around you. For example, "I can see a clock."

4 Things You Can Feel

Bring attention to and name four physical sensations. For example, "I feel my feet against the ground."

3 Things You Can Hear

Listen carefully and identify three distinct sounds. For example, "I hear birds chirping outside."

2 Things You Can Smell

Take a deep breath in and identify two scents around you. For example, "I smell a hint of fresh laundry." If you can't smell anything, recall a favorite scent in your mind.

1 Thing You Can Taste

If possible, notice any lingering taste in your mouth. If not, take a sip of a drink or imagine a favorite taste. For example, "I taste coffee."

When to use it? To ground you in the present moment if you are experiencing anxiety or panic.

SKILL 4

Urge Surfing

Strong urges can be triggered by events, thoughts, or feelings, and they can feel hard to control (for example, the urge to lash out at someone or engage in addictive behavior). Urge surfing encourages you to observe urges as temporary experiences that naturally come and go without needing to satisfy or act on them. Like a wave, the urge can rise, peak, and fall away.

1. **Observe the urge without reacting:** Direct your attention to an urge you are experiencing, such as an impulse to respond emotionally, engage in unhealthy behavior, or avoid something challenging. Where do you feel the urge in your body? Does it manifest as tension, restlessness, heat, pressure, or something else?

2. **Visualize the urge as a wave:** Like any wave, it starts small, rises, peaks, and eventually fades. You don't have to fight it or make it go away. Just observe it as it builds and then naturally subsides. Remind yourself, "This feeling is temporary. If I wait it out, it will pass."

3. **Breathe and stay present:** Focus on your breath as the urge moves through you. Take slow, steady inhales and exhales. Name what you feel; for example, "I notice restlessness in my hands and tightness in my chest." Stay curious; for example, "What happens if I just observe this urge instead of acting on it?"

4. **Let the wave pass:** Continue riding the wave of your urge, noticing how it peaks and then begins to fade on its own. Observing urges without acting on them strengthens your ability to tolerate distress and make choices that align with your values. Remember, "I don't have to act on this urge," or "Urges are temporary and will pass if I allow them to."

When to use it? When you feel a strong urge to do something you may regret, such as mindless scrolling on social media, making an impulse purchase, or using a substance to escape.

SKILL 5

Describe an Object with Facts

Describing something without judgment helps us see reality more clearly. Practice this skill to train your mind to be more present, objective, and mindful.

1. **Choose an object:** Pick something nearby—your phone, a cup, a pen, or a small item—and hold it in your hands or place it in front of you.
2. **Engage your senses:** Use your senses to notice the object.

   SIGHT: What color is it? What shape? Are there patterns or textures?

   TOUCH: Is it smooth, rough, warm, cool, soft, or firm?

   SOUND: Does it make a noise when tapped or moved?

   SMELL: Does it have a scent, or is it neutral?

3. **Describe using only facts:** Use facts to describe the object. Don't state your opinion, such as, "This is a pretty cup." Instead, list observable facts, such as, "This is a white ceramic cup with a curved handle and a smooth surface."
4. **Notice the difference:** Were you tempted to add opinions or judgments? How did it feel to stay neutral and focus on what was there?

When to use it? Any time, to help strengthen your mindfulness muscle.

Label Thoughts as Just Thoughts

Thoughts help us construct a narrative that makes sense of ourselves and our world. However, that doesn't mean thoughts are always factual. Sometimes, they offer a distorted or even completely false version of reality. This skill enables you to recognize your thoughts as mere thoughts, without allowing them to define you or dictate your actions.

1. **Bring awareness to your thoughts:** Take a few deep breaths and notice any thoughts that arise. They could be self-judgments, worries, or random ideas—let them come and go naturally without trying to change them.
2. **Label your thoughts:** When a strong or negative thought appears, practice labeling it as a thought. Instead of saying, "I'm a failure," reframe it as, "I am having the thought that I am a failure."
3. **Create distance from your thoughts:** After labeling your thought, take a deep breath and remind yourself with these three statements:

   "Just because I think it, doesn't mean it's true."

   "This is a thought, not a fact."

   "I don't have to believe or act on every thought my mind creates."

Then, gently shift your focus to your breath, surroundings, or whatever you did before the thought appeared. If the same thought returns, label it again and return to the present moment.

When to use it? When thoughts arise that feel heavy or unsettling, including negative thoughts you may have about yourself.

SKILL 7

Participate Fully in the Moment

When we are truly engaged in an activity, we enter a deep state of focus and enjoyment. This exercise can help strengthen your concentration muscles. With practice, you can feel more present in everyday moments and experience life more vividly.

1. **Pick an everyday activity:** Something you can fully participate in, such as eating a meal, taking a walk, listening to music, washing dishes, or talking with a friend.
2. **Set an intention to be present:** Before you begin, remind yourself, "I will bring my full attention to this moment," and "I will let go of distractions and immerse myself in what I am doing."
3. **Engage completely without multitasking:** As you begin the activity, commit yourself fully to it. When you walk, focus on the sensation of your feet on the ground. When you talk to someone, listen attentively without worrying about what to say next.
4. **Anchor yourself in the moment:** Observe what you can see, hear, smell, touch, and taste.
5. **Redirect distractions:** If your mind wanders, gently bring it back by reminding yourself, "Right now, I am just doing this."
6. **Reflect:** Did you feel more connected to the experience? How was this different from doing the same activity on autopilot?

When to use it? For routine activities at home or work that you wish to feel more immersed in, such as washing dishes, folding laundry, or making your bed. Or to feel fully present in social situations without feeling self-conscious or distracted.

The "How" Skills of Mindfulness

The "How" skills help us stay grounded in the present moment and respond with intention. They reduce emotional suffering by shifting from judgment and distraction to clarity and effectiveness. The three HOW skills are:

- **Nonjudgmentally:** Observe experiences without labeling them "good" or "bad." Let go of how things "should" be and accept them as they are. For example, instead of thinking, "I'm lazy for feeling tired," notice, "I feel tired right now."
- **One-Mindfully:** Doing one thing at a time with full attention in the moment. For example, when eating, focus on the taste and texture of your food instead of scrolling on your phone.
- **Effectively:** Doing what works instead of what feels "right" or "fair." For example, choose to listen and problem-solve in a disagreement instead of trying to "win" the argument.

The more you practice the How skills, the easier it becomes to navigate emotions, relationships, and challenges with awareness and confidence.

SKILL 8

Replace Judgment with Facts

We often make snap judgments that cast ourselves, others, or events in a negative light. This can make it hard to clearly understand what's going on. These skills zero in on nonjudgment, so you gain a clearer picture by replacing judgments with facts.

1. **Identify a judgmental thought:** Consider a recent situation where you judged yourself, someone else, or an event. You may have had thoughts such as "I'm so lazy" or "That person is rude."
2. **Separate opinion from fact:** What are the facts of the situation? Am I labeling or making assumptions instead of observing what happened?
3. **Reframe the thought using facts:** Instead of saying "I'm so lazy," try "I didn't do much today, and I feel frustrated about that." Instead of saying "That person is rude," try saying,

   "They interrupted me while I was speaking."
4. **Observe the impact:** Notice how reframing the thought changes how you feel. Judgments are often based on emotion, while facts help us see reality as it is.

When to use it? When you feel caught up in harsh judgments about yourself, others, or events, especially those that stir up anger or frustration.

Put Yourself in Their Shoes

Putting yourself in someone else's shoes when you're angry at them helps you understand situations more clearly. It also lowers emotional intensity and makes it easier to respond effectively rather than react impulsively.

1. **Think of a time you felt angry at someone:** A disagreement with a friend, a frustrating interaction at work, or a moment where you felt hurt or disrespected.
2. **Describe the facts:** Do this without adding opinions or assumptions; write down or think about exactly what happened. Instead of saying, "They were being selfish," try saying:

   "They didn't respond to my message for two days."

3. **Step into their shoes:** Ask yourself what they might have thought or felt in that moment. Were they stressed, distracted, or unaware? Say to yourself:

   "Maybe they weren't intentionally ignoring me, but were overwhelmed with work."

4. **Notice your shift:** You don't have to excuse the person's behavior, but observe if your anger softens when you see the situation differently.
5. **Decide how to respond:** With a more balanced view, ask yourself if you need to address this or whether approaching it with curiosity (instead of blame) improves communication.

When to use it? Reflect on a recent experience when you were upset with someone and then use it the next time you disagree with someone else.

SKILL 10

The One-Task Challenge

This one-task challenge will train your mind to stay present and engaged. Practicing this daily strengthens your ability to remain mindful, reduces stress, and helps you fully engage in life.

1. **Choose your task:** Pick an everyday activity you usually do while multi-tasking or on autopilot. Some great options are watering plants, tying your shoes, slicing fruit, petting an animal, or zipping up your jacket.
2. **Set an intention:** Before starting, take a deep breath and remind yourself:

   "I will focus only on this task" and "If my mind wanders, I will gently bring it back."

3. **Engage your senses fully:** As you perform the task, pay attention to each moment using your senses:

   SIGHT: Notice the colors, shapes, and movements involved in the task.

   TOUCH: Feel the temperature, texture, and weight of objects.

   SOUND: Listen to the subtle sounds of water running or toothbrush bristles moving.

   SMELL: Take in any scents, such as soap, fresh laundry, and coffee aroma.

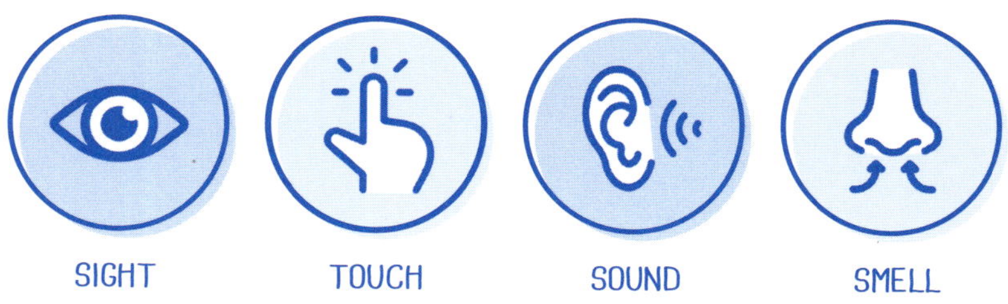

4. **Redirect distractions:** Acknowledge distractions without judgment and gently bring your focus back to the task. For example, if thoughts of your to-do list arise while washing dishes, refocus on the sensation of the warm water and the movement of your hands.

5. **Reflect on the experience:** After finishing, pause for a moment and ask yourself:

   How did it feel to focus entirely on one thing?

   Did you notice details you typically overlook?

   Was it challenging to stay present?

> **When to use it?** Make it a daily habit to practice while doing routine tasks, even for short periods of time.

SKILL 11

Mindful Eating

Mindful eating helps us slow down and stay present. It can also increase your satisfaction and awareness of hunger and fullness cues.

1. **Choose a small bite:** Pick something simple to eat, like a piece of fruit, a square of chocolate, or a cracker.
2. **Set an Intention:** Before you begin, take a deep breath and remind yourself:

   "I will fully focus on eating this bite."

3. **Observe the food:** Before taking a bite, look at the food carefully. Notice its color, shape, and texture. Hold it in your hand. What does it feel like? What is the color? Bring it close to your nose and observe the scent.
4. **Take a bite:** But don't chew immediately. Notice how it feels on your tongue. Is it smooth, rough, dry, or moist? Observe your natural urge to chew and swallow.
5. **Chew with awareness:** Chew slowly. Pay attention to the flavors, textures, and sensations. Notice how the taste evolves as you chew. Try counting how many times you chew before swallowing.
6. **Swallow and pause:** Feel the movement of swallowing. Notice the aftertaste left in your mouth. Take a deep breath before moving on to the next bite.
7. **Reflect:** After finishing, pause and ask: Did I enjoy the experience more than eating on autopilot? How did it feel to focus only on eating?

When to use it? Whenever you have time to slow down and enjoy your food.

SKILL 12

Move from "Right" to Effective

While one-upping someone during a disagreement or an argument can be satisfying, it may not help you act in a way that best achieves your goals. The following skill helps you focus on being effective instead.

1. **Recall a recent conflict or challenge:** Maybe it was an argument, a disagreement at work, or a time you insisted on fairness. For example, a disagreement with a friend where you wanted them to admit they were wrong.
2. **Identify your ultimate goal:** Ask yourself what outcome you want. Do you want to be heard, to repair the relationship, to resolve the issue? Is proving you're right the best way to achieve that?
3. **Compare "right" vs. "effective":** Consider two approaches:
   - **The "right" approach:** What would happen if you insisted on proving you were right? For example, if you told a friend they were wrong and refused to back down.
   - ✓ **The "effective" approach:** What could you do to achieve your real goal instead? For example, if you listened to your friend's perspective, expressed your feelings calmly, and worked toward understanding.
4. **Choose effectiveness:** What action would best serve your long-term goal? Can you let go of your need to be "right" if it helps to solve the problem? Ask yourself, "How can I communicate in a way that keeps the conversation productive?"

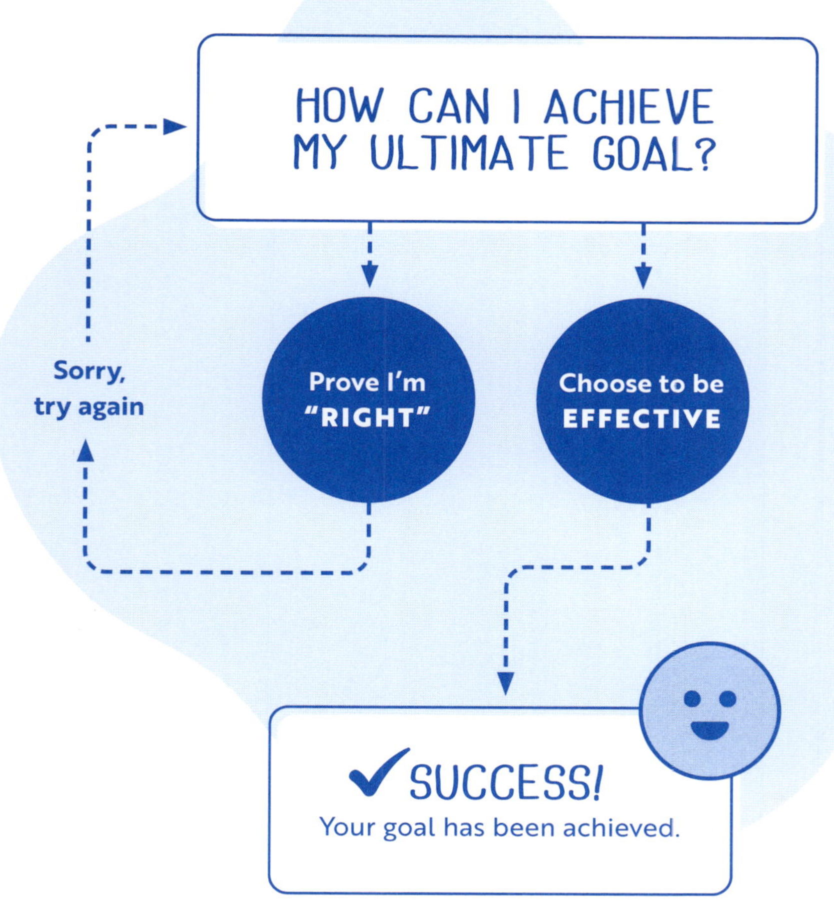

When to use it? During a disagreement or an argument with someone. Choosing effectiveness helps you maintain relationships, reduce stress, and achieve what truly matters.

SKILL 13

Loving-Kindness Meditation

This Buddhist practice uses words, feelings, and images to express goodwill and friendliness toward yourself and others. It is a powerful way to shift from judgment or anger to compassion, helping you build better relationships and inner peace.

1. **Find a comfortable position:** Sit in a quiet place where you won't be disturbed.
2. **Close your eyes:** Softly focus on a spot in front of you. Take a few slow, deep breaths, relaxing your body with each exhale.
3. **Start with yourself:** Silently repeat the following phrases, directing warmth and kindness toward yourself. Say them slowly, pausing between each one. If self-kindness is difficult, imagine how you wish happiness for a close friend and extend that kindness to yourself.

   May I be happy. May I be healthy. May I be safe. May I live with ease.

4. **Extend kindness to someone you love:** Now, bring to mind a friend, family member, or mentor. Picture them in your mind and silently say these phrases while feeling warmth and kindness radiating toward that person.

   May they be happy. May they be healthy. May they be safe. May they live with ease.

5. **Extend kindness to a neutral person:** Think of someone you don't know well—maybe a coworker, a cashier, or a neighbor. Silently repeat the phrases for them.

   May they be happy. May they be healthy. May they be safe. May they live with ease.

6. **Extend kindness to someone you struggle with:** Think of someone who has hurt you or caused frustration. Show them the same kindness. This doesn't mean excusing their behavior; instead, let go of your resentment. Choose peace over anger.

   May they be happy. May they be healthy. May they be safe. May they live with ease.

7. **Extend kindness to the world:** Finally, expand this feeling of compassion outward, sending it to all living beings:

   May they be happy. May they be healthy. May they be safe. May they live with ease.

8. **Reflect:** Take a few deep breaths. Notice how you feel—lighter, calmer, or more openhearted. Recognize that practicing kindness benefits you just as much as it does those to whom you send kindness.

> **When to use it?** When you want to feel more compassion and inner peace and have five or more minutes to spare.

Bonus Mindfulness Skills

In my own life and my work with clients, I've found that the most helpful mindfulness skills are the ones you can use in real time. I've chosen these five bonus mindfulness skills because they are quick, simple practices that can make a difference when you need them most. They are easy to apply, effective, and can be done anywhere.

These skills are designed to help with grounding, emotional regulation, self-compassion, and awareness. These are all essential elements of a mindful life. Whether you're feeling overwhelmed, caught in self-judgment, or struggling to stay present, you'll find a tool here to help.

Try them out, experiment, and find what works best for you. The more you practice, the more these skills will become second nature, making it more likely that you stay present, regulated, and resilient daily.

Five-Finger Breathing

Five-finger breathing gives you a tangible focus when anxiety, stress, or distractions take over. The more you practice, the faster and more naturally it will help you reset and refocus.

1. Hold out one hand in front of you with your fingers spread apart.
2. Use the index finger of your other hand to slowly trace along the outline of your fingers.
3. Inhale deeply as you trace up the side of one finger.
4. Exhale slowly as you trace down the other side.
5. Continue moving finger by finger, inhaling as you go up and exhaling as you go down.
6. Focus on the sensations of movement, touch, and breath. If your mind wanders, gently bring it back.
7. When you finish tracing all five fingers, take one last deep breath and notice how you feel.

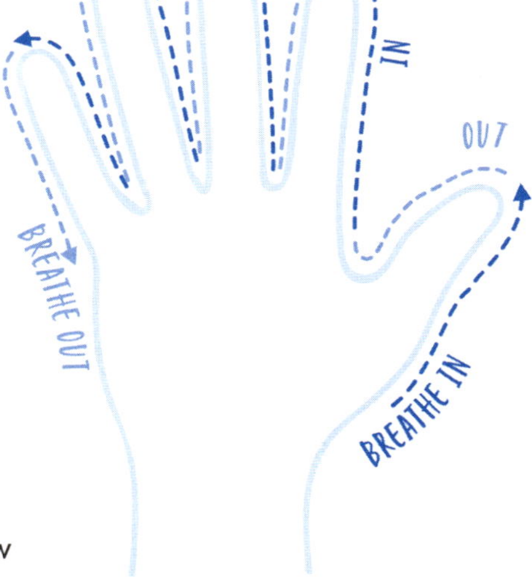

When to use it? In moments of high stress, especially when your thoughts are racing, your body feels tense or overwhelmed, and you want to quickly calm your nervous system.

SKILL 15

Speak to Yourself with Compassion

The way we talk to ourselves matters. Self-compassion is not about ignoring mistakes but treating ourselves with the kindness we'd offer a friend.

1. **Notice self-criticism:** The next time you think negatively about yourself, pause for a moment. Examples of critical thoughts include, "I always mess things up," "I'm not good enough," or "I should be doing better."
2. **Take a deep breath:** Inhale slowly through your nose, hold for a moment, and exhale through your mouth. Imagine letting go of self-judgment as you exhale.
3. **Replace the negative thought:** Instead of criticism, choose kind, validating words to support yourself, such as, "This is hard, but I'm doing my best," or "Everyone makes mistakes. I can learn from this." Say the phrase silently or out loud while breathing deeply.
4. **Repeat until it feels genuine:** Or until you think it may be true. If self-compassion feels unnatural at first, that's okay! Continue practicing; your brain will default to kindness rather than criticism over time.

When to use it? When you catch yourself speaking unkindly to yourself.

Accept Pleasant and Unpleasant Moments

Life is a mix of pleasant and unpleasant moments. Mindfulness helps you accept both without clinging or resisting, allowing you to move through life with greater ease and emotional flexibility.

1. **Set aside a few minutes at the end of your day:** Find a quiet space, take a deep breath, and reflect on your day.
2. **Identify one pleasant and one unpleasant experience:** "I had a warm cup of tea this morning and felt calm" versus "I got stuck in traffic and felt frustrated."
3. **Describe each experience mindfully:** Stick to facts, without adding judgments. Focus on what happened and how you felt, rather than labeling it as "good" or "bad."
4. **Observe your reactions:** Do this without clinging or resisting. Notice how you may want to hold on to pleasant moments and push away or dwell on unpleasant ones. Remind yourself, "Both experiences are part of life, and I can accept them as they are," and "I don't need to avoid discomfort or chase happiness; both will come and go."
5. **Breathe and let go:** Take a deep breath in...and out. Carry this balanced awareness into tomorrow.

When to use it? At the end of your day, you can reflect on your experiences.

SKILL 17

One Minute of Focus

Just sixty seconds of focused attention can help reset your mind, reduce stress, and bring you back to the present moment. It helps to set a timer on your phone or watch.

1. **Choose your focus:** Options include:

   YOUR BREATH: Pay attention to each inhale and exhale.

   A SOUND: Listen to a fan, birds, or distant traffic.

   A BODY SENSATION: Notice the feeling of your hands on your lap or your feet on the floor.

   A WORD OR PHRASE: Silently repeat a calming phrase ("I am here" or "All is well in this moment").

2. **Gently redirect when distracted:** If your mind wanders (which it will!), gently bring it back to your focus. No judgment. Just return to the present moment.

3. **Take one deep breath to end:** When the minute is up, take a slow, deep breath in...and out. Notice if you feel even slightly calmer, more grounded, or focused.

When to use it? When you have a minute to pause, reset, and be fully present—even on busy days.

MINDFULNESS SKILLS TRACKER

Train your brain to be mindful by tracking each skill used. Practice each a few times, including real-life situations. Rate the skill's usefulness instead of just checking it off:

1 = Didn't help at all.
2 = Helped a little, and I felt mindful for a while.
3 = Helped a lot.

MINDFULNESS SKILLS OF DBT	RATING				
Meet Your Wise Mind					
Wise Mind Breathing					
The "What" Skills of Mindfulness					
Leaves on a Stream					
5-4-3-2-1 Grounding					
Urge Surfing					
Describe an Object with Facts					
Label Thoughts as Just Thoughts					
Participate Fully in the Moment					
The "How" Skills of Mindfulness					
Replace Judgment with Facts					
Put Yourself in Their Shoes					
The One-Task Challenge					
Mindful Eating					
Move from "Right" to Effective					
Loving-Kindness Meditation					
Bonus Mindfulness Skills					
Five-Finger Breathing					
Speak to Yourself with Compassion					
Accept Pleasant and Unpleasant Moments					
One Minute of Focus					

SECTION 3

Skills to Handle Big Emotions

Emotions can be challenging. Pleasant emotions, such as joy, guide us toward what is meaningful in life, while others, like sadness, fear, and anger, can be messy, confusing, and sometimes overwhelming.

The third module of DBT, Emotional Regulation, equips you with skills to understand, manage, and respond to big emotions in ways that help rather than hurt you. This doesn't mean ignoring or controlling your emotions but learning to work with them instead of being overwhelmed.

Think of emotions as waves in the ocean of life. You cannot have an ocean without waves. Emotional Regulation skills help you ride the waves instead of getting pulled under. They make it easier to handle stress, make thoughtful decisions, and respond to situations in ways that align with your goals and values.

Goals of Emotional Regulation

Improving your overall mental well-being by learning how to recognize, understand, and express your emotions in a way that serves the people you love is essential. The keys to making the most of Emotional Regulation include:

- ✓ **Understand Emotions:** Learn how emotions work and why they arise.
- ✓ **Reduce Emotional Vulnerability:** Strengthen emotional resilience by caring for your body and mind.
- ✓ **Change Unhelpful Emotional Responses:** Develop strategies to shift emotional reactions when needed.
- ✓ **Increase Positive Emotions:** Build a life with more meaningful and joyful experiences.
- ✓ **Handle Difficult Emotions More Effectively:** Learn how to sit with and process emotions instead of suppressing or avoiding them.

EMOTIONAL REGULATION CHEAT SHEET

Skills to Handle Big Emotions

UNDERSTAND YOUR EMOTIONS

- Get to Know Your Emotions
- Understand Your Emotions
- Challenge Beliefs That Keep You Stuck

CHOOSE HOW TO RESPOND TO EMOTIONS

- Separate Facts from Feelings
- Check the Facts
- Take Opposite Action
- Solve a Problem

ENHANCE YOUR EMOTIONAL RESILIENCE

- Identify Your Core Values
- Define a Life Worth Living
- Take Small Steps Toward Big Goals
- Accumulate Positive Experiences
- Build Mastery
- Learn How to Cope Ahead
- PLEASE to Manage Emotions
- Improve Your Sleep Hygiene
- Ride the Wave of Emotion

Bonus Emotional Regulation Skills

- Emotion Exposure Practice
- Pros and Cons of Changing Emotions
- Avoid Avoiding
- Reinforce Positive Emotions

Understand Your Emotions

Identifying and understanding emotions is a powerful tool for change. Research shows that simply naming an emotion can reduce its intensity. Knowing your feelings makes you more likely to respond with intention rather than impulsively. This translates to fewer regretted decisions, greater emotional balance, and healthier relationships.

It's important to remember that emotions, even uncomfortable ones like anger, sadness, or fear, aren't problems to solve. They're signals. They help you recognize what you care about, what feels off, and what you may need. The trouble usually comes not from the feeling, but from how you respond.

When you ignore or push away emotions, they often show up louder, through outbursts, avoidance, or internal shutdown. But the more you learn to recognize and name your feelings, the more you can move through them skillfully and with less suffering.

Emotional awareness is a skill you can build. With practice, you can better identify emotions in the moment, understand what they're telling you, and choose what to do next.

There are no destructive emotions, just emotions asking to be understood.

Get to Know Your Emotions

The first step to regulating emotions is identifying what you're feeling. The Emotion Wheel on page 52 expands your emotional vocabulary by moving from general feelings to more precise ones. The Emotion Wheel helps you go from overwhelmed to aware! The more you can name your emotion, the easier it is to understand it and decide what to do next.

1. **Start in the center of the wheel:** Begin with one of the four core emotions in the center of the wheel: sad, mad, happy, scared. Ask yourself, "Which core emotion seems closest to what I'm feeling?"
2. **Move outward:** The second and third rings of the wheel provide more specific words to help you describe your emotion clearly. For example, from "sad" you can move to "lonely," then to "isolated."
3. **Say it or write it:** Once you find a word that fits, say it out loud or write it down. Naming emotions reduces confusion, builds self-awareness, and helps you choose the best DBT skill to use next.

CONTINUED>

Emotion Wheel

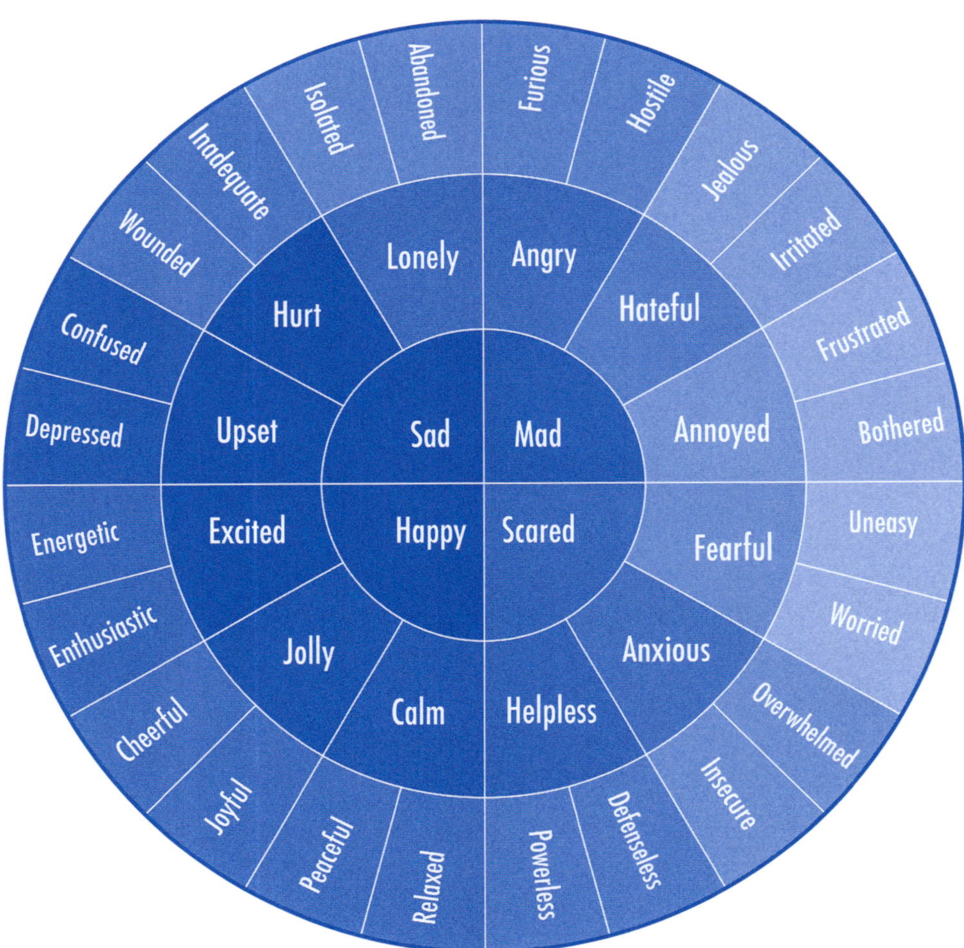

When to use it? You can return to this emotion wheel whenever your emotions are difficult to describe or when understanding your feelings is hard.

Understand Your Emotions

This exercise helps you break down a recent emotional experience to identify better what you felt, what triggered it, how it affected your body, and how you reacted. The more you understand your emotional patterns, the better you can work with them.

1. **Identify the emotion:** Choose a recent situation where you felt a strong emotion. Use the Emotion Wheel to label it. For example, "I felt __________."
2. **Identify the prompting event:** Ask yourself what happened before this feeling emerged. "I felt ______________ when ______________." For example, "I felt jealous when I saw my coworker get praised in front of the team."
3. **Notice how it felt in your body:** Did you experience a tight chest, clenched fists, butterflies in your stomach, or heat in your face? Mark where you feel it on the illustration.
4. **Identify the action urge:** What did you feel like doing? Did you want to shut down, lash out, cry, run away? For example, "I wanted to ____________________."
5. **Reflect on the pattern:** Have you felt this before in similar situations? What does it tend to lead to? For example, "This emotion usually shows up when ____________ ________________" or "It helps/hurts me by ____________________."

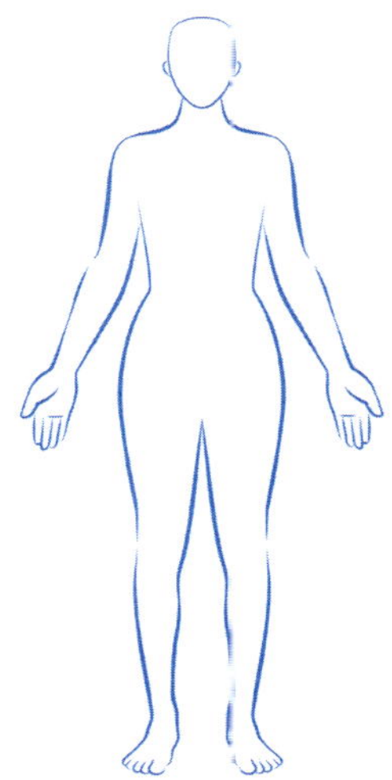

When to use it? When you want to understand better what you're feeling.

SKILL 20

Challenge Beliefs That Keep You Stuck

We all have certain rules about emotions. For example, "If I express my feelings, I'll seem weak." In DBT, we call these emotional myths, and they can keep us stuck in shame, avoidance, or impulsive behavior. This exercise involves three steps that challenge your emotional myths.

1. **Notice the myth:** Question what you're telling yourself. "What do I believe about this emotion?" "Where did that belief come from?" or "Is it helping me or hurting me?" If it sounds harsh, absolute, or shame-based, it very well might be a myth.
2. **Talk back with the truth:** If you've been telling yourself a series of myths, choose one at a time and reframe it. For example:

   MYTH: "If I feel this way, it must be true."

   REFRAME: "I'm feeling rejected, but that's a feeling, not a fact."

3. **Practice it in real time:** It will strengthen your reframing muscle.

   Name the myth.

   Say the reframe.

   Take a breath and allow space for this new truth.

Using the following chart can help you discover the right reframing for you.

EMOTIONAL MYTH	TRUTH TO TALK BACK WITH
"If I feel it, it must be true."	"Feelings are real, but they're not facts."
"Strong emotions mean I'm weak."	"Strong emotions show I care."
"I shouldn't feel this way."	"Emotions show up. I can choose my response."
"If I ignore it, it will go away."	"Avoided emotions tend to grow louder."
"Expressing emotions makes me a burden."	"Sharing feelings builds connection."
"I'll never stop feeling this."	"Emotions rise and fall."
"Others make me feel this way."	"Others may trigger me, but my emotions are mine to manage."
"Feeling emotions means losing control."	"I can feel without acting on every emotion."
"Some emotions are bad."	"Emotions are messengers, not enemies."
"I should always be happy."	"A full life includes all emotions."

You can write your own if you notice a personal myth.

When to use it? When you're judging yourself for how you feel or when a belief about emotions is making things worse.

Choose How to Respond to Emotions

Emotions are valid, meaningful, and worthy of attention. But they are not always accurate reflections of reality or helpful guides for choosing the most effective behavior in a given situation.

Sometimes our emotional reactions don't match the facts or lead to urges that conflict with our long-term goals. Learning to work with emotions, especially when they are painful, intense, or misleading, can be the difference between suffering and building a life worth living.

We can influence our emotions by responding skillfully to them. That means slowing down, checking reality, challenging assumptions, and choosing how to act based on what works, rather than what our emotions demand in the moment. We can be supported by tools that help us pause, reflect, and choose intentional responses. The skills in this section are designed to help you change how you respond to your emotions. Each skill gives you a different path toward clarity, effectiveness, and emotional growth.

SKILL 21

Separate Facts from Feelings

When emotions run high, it's easy to treat feelings like facts. This skill helps you slow down, notice your inner experience with compassion, and separate emotions from interpretations so you can respond more wisely.

1. **Start with the thought:** Name the emotionally charged thought:

   "They hate me."

2. **Identify the feeling:** What emotion is carrying this thought?

   "I feel hurt and scared."

3. **Use the camera test:** Imagine a camera recording the situation. What would it capture without judgment?

   "They haven't texted back."

4. **Compare feelings and facts:** Is your interpretation the only explanation?

   "Is there evidence for it, or could something else be happening?"

5. **Rephrase with an observing mind:** Try to separate your reaction from the actual experience:

   "I'm having the thought that they hate me" and "I'm feeling rejected, but facts don't prove that."

When to use it? When intense emotions cloud your thinking and you want clarity before responding.

SKILL 22

Check the Facts

In DBT, we often say feelings aren't facts. Emotions are authentic and valid, but they're not always accurate. The exercise helps you pause, slow down, and determine whether your emotional response fits the facts or whether assumptions, old patterns, or unhelpful thinking influence it. Once you understand if your emotion aligns, you can decide on the next step.

ASK YOURSELF THESE QUESTIONS:

1. **What is the emotion I want to change?** Naming the emotion brings awareness. You can't change what you can't identify.
2. **What is the event prompting my emotion?** Describe it using just the facts, no interpretations or assumptions. For example, "She walked by without saying hi," not, "She ignored me because she's mad at me."
3. **Am I interpreting the situation correctly?** What else could be true? Could stress, distraction, or a misunderstanding explain their behavior?
4. **Am I thinking in extremes?** Watch for black-and-white thoughts like, "They always ignore me," "This will ruin everything," or "They hate me." Seek a more balanced or flexible perspective.
5. **What is the actual likelihood of the worst-case scenario?** Is that scenario possible? Likely? Or just scary? Often, our fear inflates the risk.
6. **If the worst did happen, could I cope?** Imagine saying to yourself, "It would be hard, but I could handle it." Visualize yourself using coping skills and support to get through.
7. **What next?** If the emotion doesn't fit the facts, try to **Take Opposite Action** (page 60) or use mindfulness skills. If the emotion does fit the facts, try to **Solve a Problem** (page 62) to take effective action.

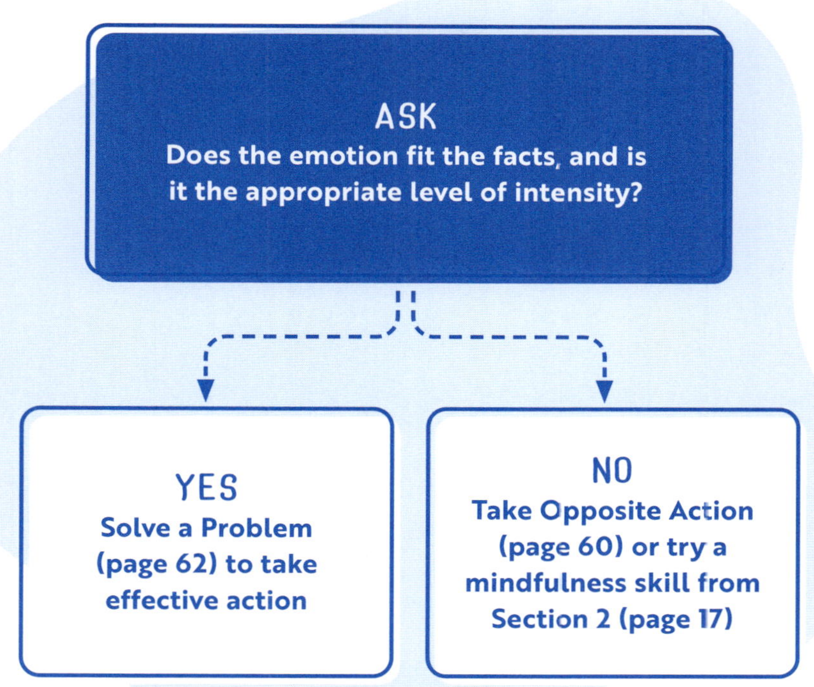

When to use it? When your emotions tell you something, but you're unsure if it matches the situation.

SKILL 23

Take Opposite Action

Opposite Action helps you shift your emotions by doing the opposite of what they are urging you to do. If sadness tells you to isolate, go out and connect. If fear says avoid, gently lean in. If anger says lash out, slow down and walk away. The key to making it work is going all the way. This means shifting your behavior, facial expression, tone of voice, and body posture.

1. **Identify the emotion and the urge:** Name how you feel and what that feeling urges you to do. Be specific.
2. **Does the urge help or hurt?** Does this emotion fit the facts of the situation? Even if it does, would acting on this urge help or hurt you? If it will make things worse, or doesn't fit the facts, Opposite Action is your move.
3. **Do the opposite:** Use your voice, body, and energy. Fully commit to the opposite behavior. Smile and make eye contact if you are afraid or ashamed. Speak gently and walk away if your urge is to explode with anger. Engage with others if your urge is to isolate.

The following table will help you quickly identify your feelings and urges and choose an effective opposite action.

EMOTION	ACTION URGE	OPPOSITE ACTION
Anger	Attack, yell	Gently express, walk away
Sadness	Withdraw, isolate	Engage, move, connect
Fear	Avoid, flee, freeze	Approach the feared situation safely
Shame	Hide, shrink, self-blame	Hold your head high, face up to it
Jealousy	Check, control, cling	Let go of checking, give space
Guilt	Over-apologize, avoid	Make amends once, then engage normally
Envy	Compare to others, resent	Practice gratitude, celebrate others

When to use it? When you're feeling a strong emotion that doesn't fit the facts, or when your action urge would be ineffective or harmful, even if the emotion itself is valid.

SKILL 24

Solve a Problem

Sometimes, you might be so overwhelmed by a problem that you feel unable to solve it. When this happens, you can work on shifting from overwhelm to action. You don't need to solve everything at once, but these six steps are a great place to start.

1. **Calm your body:** Take slow, deep breaths. Emotion Mind makes clear thinking harder.
2. **Describe the problem clearly:** Stick to facts, not fears or blame. Example:

   "I haven't responded to that email, and it's stressing me out."
3. **Identify your goal:** What do you want to be different? Example:

   "I want to respond calmly" or "I want to stop repeating the same argument."
4. **Brainstorm solutions:** List all ideas, even weird ones.
5. **Pick a solution and plan it:** What will you do? When? What support do you need?
6. **Try it, then evaluate:** Did anything improve? If not, try another idea.

When to use it? When your emotion is linked to a real problem, action can help.

Enhance Your Emotional Resilience

When the Emotion Mind takes over, it's hard to think clearly, make effective choices, or respond in a way that aligns with our values. When you're tired, stressed, sick, or stretched too thin, emotions tend to hit harder and stick around. Unmet physical or emotional needs weaken our ability to cope, making even small challenges feel like too much. The good news is that we can reduce emotional vulnerability by taking care of our bodies and minds and by building lives that align with what matters most to us.

The DBT skills in this section aim to enhance your emotional resilience. You'll discover ways to boost confidence, manage stress, practice self-care, and establish long-term emotional balance. By reducing vulnerability, you can build a strong foundation so that when emotions arise, you are prepared to handle them skillfully.

SKILL 25

Identify Your Core Values

Understanding what matters most helps you navigate life with intention even when you are experiencing strong emotions. Underline the values that are important to you. Then, circle three to five central to your vision for the life you wish to lead. Add your own values at the end of this chart if they are not on the list!

Authenticity	Being real, honest, and authentic to yourself
Balance	Finding harmony between work, rest, and play
Connection	Deep, meaningful relationships with others
Contribution	Helping others and making a positive impact
Creativity	Expressing yourself through art, writing, ideas, or innovation
Curiosity	Asking questions, exploring, and being open to new ideas
Freedom	Living according to your beliefs without feeling trapped
Growth	Learning, evolving, and pushing past comfort zones
Health	Caring for your physical and emotional well-being
Independence	Standing on your own and making your own decisions
Integrity	Acting in line with your values, even when it's hard

Joy	Making space for fun, playfulness, and laughter
Justice	Standing up for fairness and equality
Kindness	Treating yourself and others with care and compassion
Peace	Creating calm in your environment and inner world
Purpose	Contributing to something meaningful
Resilience	Bouncing back from difficulty with strength and flexibility
Self-respect	Honoring your worth and treating yourself with dignity
Spirituality	Feeling connected to something greater than yourself

For each core value you identify, ask yourself how you would live your life according to this value. Turn the answer into a small, specific goal. For example, if the value is connection, you can set the goal of reaching out to a good friend once a week.

When to use it? When you feel stuck, overwhelmed, or uncertain about a decision

SKILL 26

Define a Life Worth Living

Building a life worth living starts with knowing what kind of life you want. This exercise can help you ride out the tough times and recall the possibility of a life with joy, connection, and achievement. You'll need a journal or writing paper for this.

1. **What does a life worth living mean to you?** Close your eyes and imagine your life in five years, where everything has worked out as you wanted. What would that life look like?

2. **Write about it:** Answer these questions:

   How would my life reflect my values?

   What would I spend my time doing?

   What choices might I be making?

   Who would be in my life?

3. **Refine your life worth living:** Write a statement that describes what it looks like to you. For example, "My life worth living would be to have a strong and loving relationship with my child, a safe and pleasant living space, caring and fun friendships, a stable income, and time to do creative things just for fun."

When to use it? If you feel disconnected, aimless, or unsure of what matters most in your life.

Take Small Steps Toward Big Goals

Significant life changes happen through small actions. Every intentional step brings you closer to a life that feels more like your own, helping you build confidence and add meaning to your day. This skill allows you to break your long-term goals into manageable, achievable actions that you can take now.

1. **Choose one long-term goal to work on:** Look back at your values-based goals, such as "Build deeper friendships."
2. **Identify a small, concrete action you can take now:** Make it simple and realistic, such as texting a friend to check in, decluttering one small area, trying one new recipe, or taking a screen break for an hour.
3. **Plan it:** What will you do? When will you do it? What might get in the way? How can you handle that?
4. **Check in at the end of the action:** Did it help you feel more connected to your life goals? What's one more step you can take next?

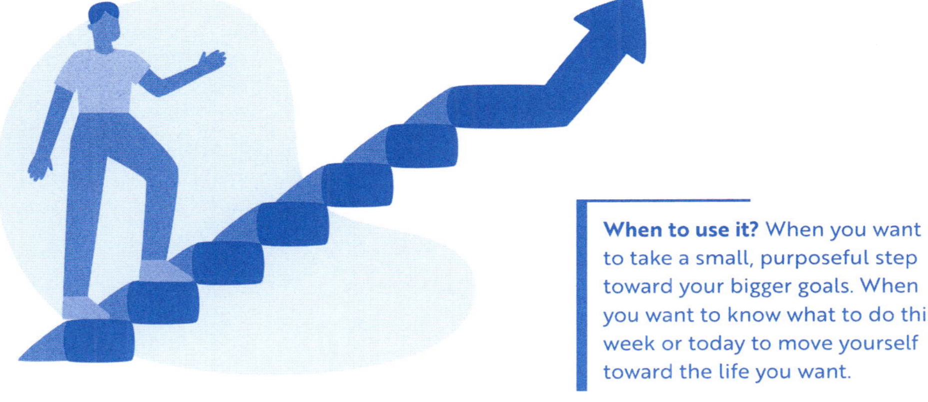

When to use it? When you want to take a small, purposeful step toward your bigger goals. When you want to know what to do this week or today to move yourself toward the life you want.

SKILL 28

Accumulate Positive Experiences

This exercise emphasizes creating enjoyable moments for yourself instead of waiting for joy to appear by chance. These small, meaningful experiences elevate your emotional baseline, making you more balanced and resilient when difficult emotions arise. The more you incorporate them into your life, the more grounded, balanced, and resilient you will feel.

1. **Identify what feels pleasant:** List small activities that bring peace, satisfaction, or joy. Examples:

   NATURE: Sitting in the sun

   CONNECTION: Sending a kind text

   CREATIVITY: Journaling, baking

   RELAXATION: Warm shower, stretching, music

   COMFORT: Cuddling a pet, soft clothes

2. **Plan pleasant events:** Pick one to three activities this week. Add them to your calendar appointments. Examples:

   "Walk after lunch Tuesday."

   "Listen to music Thursday evening."

   "Send a thank-you text Saturday."

3. **Be present for the pleasant:** Notice sights, sounds, and sensations. Let yourself enjoy the moment without guilt. Remind yourself that joy is vital to your mental health.

When to use it? When life feels heavy, or even when things are okay. Building joy now creates emotional strength for later.

SKILL 29

Build Mastery

It is crucial to engage in consistent actions, big or small, that nurture a sense of competence and capability, especially in areas that matter to you. Mastery builds momentum. The more you succeed in overcoming challenges, the more confident and emotionally stable you become.

1. **Identify something you want to improve or practice:** Anything from cooking, organizing, social skills, movement, self-care, studying, or time management.
2. **Start small and doable:** Pick something slightly challenging, but realistic. Treat it like a real commitment. Examples include walking twice this week, trying a new recipe, or practicing mindfulness for a week straight.
3. **Track and reflect:** At the end of the week, assess whether you followed through. What did you notice or learn? Remember, success builds with repetition.

When to use it? When you feel helpless, stuck, or like you're falling behind. Or anytime you want to grow your confidence and capability through small, steady wins.

SKILL 30

Learn How to Cope Ahead

Visualizing a situation and rehearsing how you will respond helps you decrease the risk of feeling overwhelmed and increase the likelihood of applying your skills when it matters. The more you practice success, the more capable you will be in handling difficult moments with skill and intention.

1. **Identify a challenging situation:** Pick an upcoming event that might be emotionally hard. Examples: A tough conversation, a test, a doctor visit, or being around a triggering person.
2. **Visualize it clearly:** Close your eyes and walk through the event from start to finish. Picture where you are, what's happening, and what you feel.
3. **Rehearse skillful coping:** Mentally practice using skills, like DEAR MAN (page 124) or TIPP with Paced Breathing (page 94), especially if you expect distress or conflict.
4. **Plan ahead:** What can you do now to support yourself? Prep notes? Bring a calming object? Schedule support after?

When to use it? Anytime you know something hard is coming and want to face it with skills instead of panic.

PLEASE to Manage Emotions

Neglecting basic self-care increases our chances of feeling emotionally off-balance. This exercise reminds us that the mind and body are deeply connected. Caring for your physical health, even in small ways, can reduce emotional vulnerability and enhance your ability to use DBT skills effectively.

Treat Physical iLlness Take care of your body. Follow up on symptoms, take medications as prescribed, and rest when needed.

Eat well: Balanced meals and regular snacks help stabilize energy and mood. Skipping meals = more mood swings.

Avoid mood-altering substances: Alcohol and drugs can cloud thinking and intensify emotions. Notice their effects and reduce use when emotionally vulnerable.

Sleep enough: Lack of sleep fuels emotional reactivity. Aim for a regular sleep schedule and seven to nine hours a night.

Exercise more: Even a few minutes of movement, like walking, stretching, or dancing, can reduce stress and help regulate emotions.

When to use it? When you're emotionally vulnerable, irritable, or overwhelmed. When you want to strengthen your foundation for handling emotions skillfully or reduce your vulnerability to negative emotions. This skill is *always* a good idea!

SKILL 32

Improve Your Sleep Hygiene

When you're sleep-deprived, your brain becomes more reactive, your stress tolerance diminishes, and even minor issues can feel overwhelming. Sleep hygiene involves developing habits and creating an environment that fosters deep, consistent rest.

1. **Set a consistent sleep schedule:** Wake up and sleep at the same time daily, even on weekends. A regular rhythm helps your body fall asleep more easily.
2. **Create a wind-down routine:** Start relaxing thirty to sixty minutes before bed. Try screen-free activities like reading, stretching, gentle yoga, a warm bath, or calming music to signal to your brain that it's time to rest.
3. **Optimize your environment:** Keep your room cool, dark, and quiet. Use blackout curtains, white noise, or an eye mask. Reserve your bed for sleep and sex, not worry.
4. **Avoid sleep disruptors:** Limit caffeine, nicotine, alcohol, and screens before bed. If you can't fall asleep after twenty to thirty minutes, get up, do something calming, and try again.

When to use it? Better sleep habits = better emotional resilience. Pro tip: Can't stop ruminating? Splash cold water on your face (TIPP skill 40, p. 92), then try paced breathing (TIPP skill 42, page 94).

SKILL 33

Ride the Wave of Emotion

By observing an emotion mindfully and allowing it to pass on its own, you reduce suffering and build emotional strength. Most emotional responses only last about ninety seconds unless we feed them with thoughts or judgments. If you let it, the wave will pass.

1. **Name the emotion:** Gently label what you're feeling as if you're narrating a story, without judgment or drama. For example, "Sadness is here." "I'm noticing fear." "Anger is rising." This helps create a little distance from the emotion.
2. **Observe urges:** But don't act. Sadness might urge you to isolate. Anger might encourage you to yell. Fear might advise you to flee. Notice the urge without reacting. You're watching the wave, not getting swept away.
3. **Tune in to the body:** Where do you feel the emotion? Chest? Gut? Shoulders?
4. **Just notice.** Breathe into those places. You're observing, not fixing.
5. **Breathe and let go of control:** Take slow, steady breaths. Visualize yourself on a surfboard, breathing through the swell. Remind yourself that this emotion is not dangerous. "I can feel it without acting on it. It will pass."
6. **Experience it, then watch it fade:** Don't suppress it. Don't amplify it. Don't chase it. Just be with it until it naturally peaks and fades.

When to use it? When you're experiencing an intense emotion and feel the urge to escape, suppress, or act impulsively to make it disappear. This allows you to process an emotion by feeling it, without feeding it or distracting from it, and then letting it pass.

Bonus Emotional Regulation Skills

When emotions feel tangled, confusing, or stuck, the Standard DBT skills may not be enough. This section includes bonus Emotional Regulation tools I often teach in therapy and use in my own life. They are practical, accessible skills that go beyond the basics and offer new ways to work with emotions that linger, intensify, or resist change.

These tools can help you overcome emotional avoidance; understand the purpose behind what you're feeling; and build resilience through small, meaningful moments of connection, insight, or joy. Whether you're struggling to let go of an emotion that's overstayed its welcome, finding it hard to face a feeling you usually avoid, or just needing to reinforce your emotional "wins," these practices support you. Reach for these extra tools when you feel stuck, overwhelmed, or unsure of what comes next.

Emotion Exposure Practice

Every time you face a feeling, you regain your power to live a fuller, freer life. Over time, emotions lose their ability to scare you, and you gain confidence to manage your feelings no matter what life throws at you.

1. **Choose an emotion you avoid:** Pick a feeling you tend to push away, like grief, shame, fear, or anger. Ask yourself, "What emotion feels too big to face?"
2. **Find a safe way to approach it:** Start small. Examples include looking at a photo that brings up grief, reading an old journal entry, or imagining a tough conversation.
3. **Feel the emotion for five minutes:** Set a timer and let yourself feel the emotion. Breathe. Say, "This is hard, but I'm safe. This feeling will pass."
4. **Ride the wave:** Let the feeling rise and fall. Don't fix, avoid, or feed it; just feel it without judgment.
5. **Soothe and reflect:** Afterward, use a calming activity. What did you learn about your ability to tolerate this feeling?

When to use it? When you're avoiding a feeling. If you are in therapy, this is a great skill to try for the first time during a session.

SKILL 35

Pros and Cons of Changing Emotions

Emotions often feel *right*, even when they're painful. Anger feels empowering. Sadness honors what was lost. Fear is about protection. When you experience these emotions, it's good to pause and determine if you're moving forward or getting stuck. Weighing the pros and cons of your feelings gives you back the power to choose what's best for you.

1. **Identify the emotion you're holding on to:** Name what you're feeling. Then ask, "What about this emotion feels hard to let go of, even if it's hurting me?"
2. **Acknowledge the benefits of holding on:** This is where we honor the emotional truth. Ask, "What does this emotion do for me?" Examples include, "Anger makes me feel powerful." "Sadness connects me to what I've lost." "Fear keeps me from risking more pain." Just notice, without judgment, what the emotion is doing for you.
3. **Explore the costs of holding on:** Is this emotion hurting your relationships, peace, or health? For example, "Staying angry keeps me tense and isolated from others." "Fear is causing me to shrink my world to what feels safe," or "Sadness is stopping me from connecting."
4. **Weigh the trade-offs:** Try one or all of these reflections to reframe and consider another perspective. Then ask yourself, "Would changing this emotion help me live a life that feels more like what I want?"

HOLDING ON...	BUT IT ALSO...
Feels familiar	Keeps me stuck
Validates my pain	Hurts my relationships
Protects me	Stops me from healing

Choose a skill to support change (if you're ready). Try:

- Take Opposite Action, page 60 (acting opposite to the urge)
- Ride the Wave of Emotion, page 73 (mindfully experiencing, then letting go)
- Self-Validate to Honor Your Own Feelings, page 136 (replacing pain with kindness and understanding)

If you're not ready to try a skill, that's okay, too. Simply being aware of the cost/benefit is powerful.

When to use it? When you're caught in a painful emotion that feels justified, but it's also making your life harder and keeping you from achieving your goals.

SKILL 36

Avoid Avoiding

Avoidance provides short-term relief but leads to long-term pain. You weaken fear's grip and build your confidence whenever you confront rather than avoid. This skill allows you to face what you've been avoiding gently and mindfully, taking small steps.

1. **Notice what you're avoiding:** Ask, "What am I avoiding right now?" It could be a task, a conversation, or even a feeling, like sadness or shame.
2. **Understand the cost:** Avoidance feels safe, but it often leads to guilt, stress, missed opportunities, or consequences that increase suffering.
3. **Take small steps:** For example, avoiding a phone call.

   STEP 1: Write what you want to say.

   STEP 2: Read it out loud to yourself.

   STEP 3: Role-play the conversation with someone you trust.

   STEP 4: Make the call.

4. **Approach the first step mindfully:** Breathe and name the emotion. Say, "Avoiding keeps me stuck. Facing it helps me move forward." Then take action.
5. **Soothe and reflect:** Afterward, praise and comfort yourself. Ask, "What did I learn? What strength did I show?"

> **When to use it?** When avoidance is holding you back from something that matters.

Reinforce Positive Emotions

Whether it's pride after finishing something hard, a quiet moment of calm, or shared laughter, reinforcing positive emotions builds resilience and strengthens your capacity to ride out tougher feelings.

1. **Notice a positive emotion in the moment:** Pause when you feel calm, proud, joyful, connected. For example,

   "This tea is comforting." "I feel proud I made that call."

2. **Stretch it out and savor it:** Let the feeling last. Say, "I earned this calm." "This is joy." Stay with it for a few extra breaths.
3. **Name it and celebrate it:** Label the emotion. Acknowledge the win, big or small. Write it down, share it, or smile.
4. **Build a tool kit:** Make a list of activities that spark joy, such as listening to music, being in nature, or sending a kind message to someone, and refer to it often.
5. **Reflect at the end of each day:** End your day asking:

   "What felt good today?" or "What am I proud of?"

When to use it? Anytime you want to boost your mood, feel more balanced, or grow your emotional strength.

EMOTIONAL REGULATION SKILLS TRACKER

Using Emotional Regulation skills regularly will help you manage your emotions instead of being managed by them. Use the following scale to rate how well each skill helps regulate your emotions each time you try it.

Rating: 1 = Didn't help at all 2 = Helped a little 3 = Helped a lot

EMOTIONAL REGULATION SKILLS OF DBT	RATING				
Understand Your Emotions					
Get to Know Your Emotions					
Understand Your Emotions					
Challenge Beliefs That Keep You Stuck					
Choose How to Respond to Emotions					
Separate Facts from Feelings					
Check the Facts					
Take Opposite Action					
Solve a Problem					
Enhance Your Emotional Resilience					
Identify Your Core Values					
Define a Life Worth Living					
Take Small Steps Toward Big Goals					
Accumulate Positive Experiences					
Build Mastery					
Learn How to Cope Ahead					
PLEASE to Manage Emotions					
Improve Your Sleep Hygiene					
Ride the Wave of Emotion					

EMOTIONAL REGULATION SKILLS OF DBT	RATING				
Bonus Emotional Regulation Skills					
Emotion Exposure Practice					
Pros and Cons of Changing Emotions					
Avoid Avoiding					
Reinforce Positive Emotions					

SECTION 4

Skills to Cope with Distress

Sometimes emotions can feel overwhelming. You might feel the urge to lash out, shut down, be numb, avoid what's in front of you, or do something you might later regret. These urges are entirely human, but acting on them can make matters worse.

DBT provides a set of skills known as Distress Tolerance. They are most effective when life becomes challenging, so much so that relying on the Emotional Regulation skills from the previous section is not enough. The skills described here won't solve your problems, but they can help you endure painful moments without making the situation worse.

Distress Tolerance helps you pause and stay grounded instead of reacting and spinning out. You learn to ride out the storm until it passes.

Goals of Distress Tolerance

This section teaches you how to tolerate emotional pain when it's too late to fix the situation but too early to give up. You'll find skills to distract, soothe, accept, and anchor yourself so you can stay safe and respond wisely, even when everything feels out of control.

- ✓ **Survive the moment without making it worse:** Get through intense emotional pain or crisis without turning to impulsive or self-destructive behaviors.
- ✓ **Ride out emotional storms:** Develop the ability to sit with discomfort until it passes—because it will pass.
- ✓ **Accept reality as it is:** Reduce suffering by learning to stop fighting things that cannot change in the moment.
- ✓ **Build confidence in your coping:** Increase trust in handling challenging moments skillfully and with self-respect.
- ✓ **Create space for wise action:** Take a pause and respond with smart choices.

DISTRESS TOLERANCE CHEAT SHEET

Skills to Cope with Distress

UNDERSTANDING DISTRESS

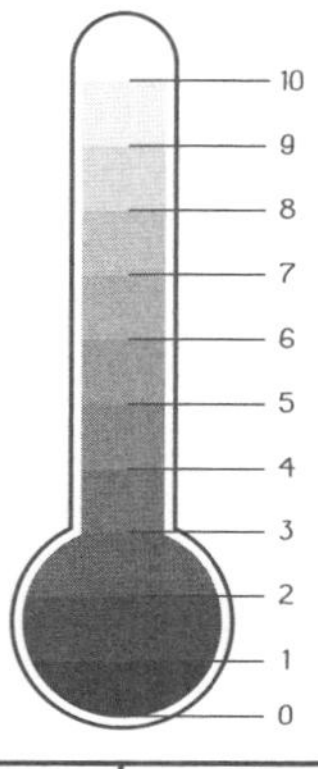

The Subjective Units of Distress Scale (SUDS) helps you measure distress from 0 (low) to 10 (high).

CRISIS SURVIVAL SKILLS

- STOP to Create Space
- Pros and Cons of Crisis Urges
- TIPP with Temperature
- TIPP with Intense Exercise
- TIPP with Paced Breathing
- TIPP with Paired Muscle Relaxation
- Wise Mind ACCEPTS
- Self-Soothe with Your Senses
- Body Scan Meditation
- IMPROVE the Moment

RADICAL ACCEPTANCE

- Practice Radical Acceptance
- Turn the Mind
- Embrace Willingness
- Half-Smiling
- Willing Hands
- Mindfulness of Current Thoughts

Bonus Distress Tolerance Skills

- Alternative Rebellion
- Build Your Distress Tolerance Kit
- On-the-Go Distress Tolerance Kit
- Crisis Survival Flowchart

Understanding Distress

Emotional distress is a normal part of life, but when it gets intense, it can be hard to know what to do in the moment. Awareness can help. One of the best tools for gauging your distress is the Subjective Units of Distress Scale (SUDS), which helps you rate your distress from 0 to 10. The scale is subjective, meaning your number is based on how you feel, not how others think you should feel or how you think others would feel in the same situation.

Knowing your SUDS score helps you match your distress level with the right DBT skills.

- **At high levels (6 or above),** distress tolerance skills are your best bet. These help you survive the moment without making things worse.
- **At low levels (0 to 5),** it's a great time to build emotional strength using Emotional Regulation and Interpersonal Effectiveness skills.

Try checking your SUDS score several times a day, especially during stressful moments.

You don't have to wait until you're overwhelmed to use DBT skills. Knowing your SUDS score helps you act wisely, early, and effectively.

How are you feeling?

Crisis Survival Skills

A crisis is when your emotions feel so intense that they might push you toward impulsive, self-destructive, or ineffective behavior.

In DBT, we define a crisis not as a life catastrophe, but as any moment when it's hard to cope without doing something that makes things worse. A crisis can occur after the death of a loved one (whether a family member, a friend, or a pet), breaking up with a romantic partner, losing a job, being lectured by your boss, being bullied or humiliated, failing an important exam, facing significant money or legal problems, or receiving scary health news.

Crisis survival skills are short-term tools designed to help you overcome a wave of distress without making it bigger. They help you pause, ride out the emotional storm, and reduce intensity just enough to stay in control.

This section offers high-impact strategies and gentler distractions that help when things feel too intense. Use them when your emotional temperature is high and your Wise Mind feels out of reach. Practice them now so you can rely on them when you need them most.

STOP to Create Space

The exercise creates space between your feeling and your response so you can act from your Wise Mind, not your Emotion Mind. STOP to Create Space gives you the gift of a pause so you can reclaim your power to act with intention instead of impulse.

Stop. Freeze. Don't speak. Don't move. Don't make that call, send that message, or answer back in that tone. Just stop.

Take a step back. Take one slow breath. Then another. You might take a step back or mentally pause. Give yourself a beat to separate from the intense emotions.

Observe. Notice what's happening within and around you. What are your thoughts, feelings, body sensations, and urges? What's going on around you? Gather data about what is happening, not what your judgments, assumptions, or automatic thoughts tell you.

Proceed mindfully. Now that you've created space, choose your next action with intention. Ask yourself what the most effective action is right now. What aligns with your values or long-term goals?

When to use it? When you're in a high-emotion moment, use STOP to avoid saying or doing something impulsive.

SKILL 39

Pros and Cons of Crisis Urges

Taking the time to weigh the pros and cons of acting on an urge gives you the space to choose wisely, even in the heat of the moment. Creating a pros and cons list for specific urges or behaviors can also be incredibly helpful before you're in crisis. When you're in Wise Mind, you can make a list to reflect on later, during moments of high emotion. By considering the pros and cons, you are giving yourself time to select a values-based response instead of reacting impulsively.

1. **Identify the urge:** What do you usually like doing when you're overwhelmed? Examples include yelling, self-harm, shutting down, bingeing, quitting something important, etc.
2. **To act or not to act:** Use the chart on this page to explore the urge from both angles. I have offered examples, but you can use the blank space in the chart to write your own notes.
3. **Look at the big picture:** Ask which choice helps you move toward a life you want. Do you want short-term relief or long-term effectiveness?
4. **Choose a skillful action:** Use the info in your table to guide your next step. Choose a distress tolerance skill (your preferred TIPP skill from pages 91–95, or Self-Soothe with Your Senses on page 97) to overcome the urge without acting on it.

	ACT ON THE URGE	DON'T ACT ON THE URGE
Pros	Example: "I'll feel immediate relief."	Example: "I'll feel proud later."
Cons	Example: "I might feel worse afterward."	Example: "The emotion might stick around longer."

TIPP YOUR BODY CHEMISTRY

Using skills that calm your nervous system reduces the physical symptoms associated with stress, like rapid heartbeat, and eases you into a state where you can use other coping skills.

In DBT, these are called the **TIPP** skills because they "tip" your body chemistry away from a fight-or-flight reaction (when your body prepares to protect you or run away from danger) and toward relaxation. The letters of the acronym can help you remember the techniques to use:

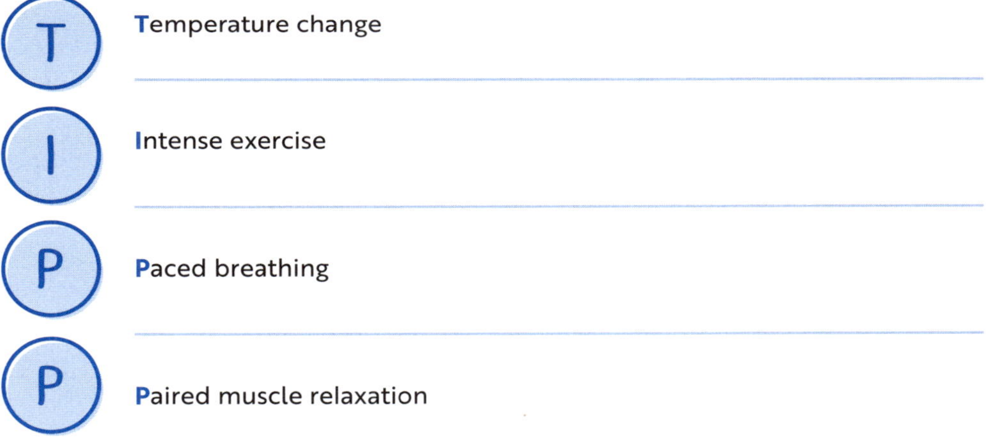

Temperature change

Intense exercise

Paced breathing

Paired muscle relaxation

In the following pages, you'll learn how to try these steps.

When to use it? When you're overwhelmed and tempted to act on an urge that may cause harm or create long-term consequences.

SKILL 40

TIPP with Temperature

The "T" in TIPP uses cold temperature to activate the dive reflex, a built-in survival response. It can be triggered when cold hits your face, especially around the eyes, forehead, and cheeks. The body responds by slowing the heart rate, reducing blood pressure, and calming the fight-or-flight system.

Safety note: This skill affects your heart rate and blood pressure. Check with your doctor before using it if you have any heart, blood pressure, or other medical conditions (especially eating disorders).

1. **Option 1: Ice dive:** Fill a bowl with cold water and ice cubes. Hold your breath and submerge your face (especially your eyes and cheeks) for fifteen to thirty seconds. Repeat one to three times if needed.
2. **Option 2: Ice pack:** Place a cold pack/compress or plastic bag of ice on your eyes and upper cheeks. Hold for thirty to sixty seconds while breathing slowly.
3. **Option 3: Frozen washcloth or cold gel eye mask:** Wrap a frozen washcloth around your face or wear a cold gel eye mask.

When to use it? When you're emotionally overwhelmed and need fast physical relief. This skill is invaluable during panic, rage, or intense anxiety.

SKILL 41

TIPP with Intense Exercise

The "I" in TIPP stands for intense exercise. By doing an intense burst of body movement, you reduce the strength of an intense emotion and release its grip on your body. You're not just exercising, you're taking charge of your nervous system in the moment.

1. **Do something that gets your heart rate up fast:** Choose an activity you can safely do for thirty seconds to a few minutes: jumping jacks, running in place, dancing it out, fast-paced walking, jogging or sprinting, shadowboxing or punching a pillow, or stair climbing.
2. **Make it count:** Move hard and fast enough that you notice your heart rate increasing and your breathing becoming heavier. The goal is to mimic a physical stress release, so your body can reset after the emotional surge.
3. **Cool down:** Afterward, do something grounding to return to calm. Try slow breathing or a body scan.

When to use it? When your emotions feel physically overwhelming, like you're about to explode, shut down, or panic.

SKILL 42

TIPP with Paced Breathing

Strong emotions trigger the body's fight-or-flight response: Your heart races, your breathing speeds up, and your muscles tense. This is your nervous system's way of preparing for danger, even if no threat exists. The first "P" in TIPP stands for paced breathing, which helps reverse your body's response by activating the parasympathetic nervous system (also known as "rest and digest"), which helps you feel safe and calm.

To practice paced breathing, follow this four/six breathing pattern.

1. Inhale gently through your nose for four seconds.
2. Pause briefly.
3. Exhale slowly through your mouth for six seconds.
4. Repeat for one or two minutes (or longer if it feels helpful).

SOME TIPS:

- Focus on making your exhale longer than your inhale. This is what turns on the calming system.
- Rest a hand on your belly and feel it rise and fall.
- If your mind wanders, gently return to the rhythm of your breath.

When to use it? When you're flooded with intense emotion, like anxiety, fear, anger, or panic, and you need to calm your body and mind quickly.

TIPP with Paired Muscle Relaxation

The second "P" in TIPP stands for Paired Muscle Relaxation, a skill that pairs slow, intentional breathing with the tensing and relaxing of different muscle groups. The goal is to reduce physical tension so that your nervous system gets the message that it's safe to relax.

1. **Get ready:** Sit or lie down in a comfortable position. Take one deep breath in and out.
2. **Tense and release:** Starting with your feet and moving upward (legs, belly, arms, face), inhale and tense a muscle group for five seconds. Exhale slowly and release the tension. Silently say: "Relax." You can do this from head to toe or just focus on a few key areas.

When to use it? When you're feeling tense, panicky, or angry, and want to calm your body quickly. In a rush? Clench your fists, squeeze your eyes shut, or tighten your shoulders, then release with a long exhale. You can feel calmer in thirty seconds.

SKILL 44

Wise Mind ACCEPTS

Wise Mind ACCEPTS are distraction tools that help you get through emotional storms without reacting impulsively. The goal isn't to eliminate your pain or fix the situation; it's to give yourself time to reach your Wise Mind.

Activities: Do something that requires focus: draw, walk, organize, play a game.

Contributing: Help someone else. Send a kind message, volunteer, or offer support.

Comparisons: Think of someone who has faced something more challenging and how you're handling this better than you might have in the past.

Emotions: Create new emotions on purpose. Watch something funny or listen to uplifting music.

Pushing Away: Set the problem aside in your mind. Visualize putting it on a shelf.

Thoughts: Distract your brain by counting backward, reciting lyrics, or naming animals alphabetically.

Sensations: Use your senses. Hold ice, smell something with a strong scent, or splash cold water.

> **When to use it?** When you're overwhelmed with emotion and must avoid acting on urges that could worsen things.

Self-Soothe with Your Senses

Self-soothing is about intentionally comforting yourself using your five senses. It's a way to remind your brain and body that you are safe, even in distress. This skill shifts your focus from emotional overwhelm to sensory grounding, creating a calming experience in the here and now.

Sight: Surround yourself with beauty or calming visuals. Light a candle, look at nature, watch clouds, flip through art books, or browse soothing photos.

Sound: Create peace or positive emotion using sound. Listen to calming music, nature sounds, white noise, or a podcast with a comforting voice.

Smell: Scents can quickly shift emotional states. Use essential oils or light incense, smell fresh herbs or citrus, or bake something familiar.

Taste: Let yourself mindfully enjoy something tasty. Sip tea, savor a piece of chocolate, eat something with texture or flavor that you enjoy slowly and attentively.

Touch: Comfort yourself with physical sensations. Wrap in a soft blanket, take a warm bath, pet an animal, hold something smooth or textured in your hands.

When to use it? When you're overwhelmed, emotionally raw, or need grounding after a distressing experience.

SKILL 46

Body Scan Meditation

This simple mindfulness practice guides your attention through your body, focusing on one area at a time. It isn't about relaxing on command; it's about noticing what's happening inside you with curiosity and compassion. You don't have to solve anything; just notice. Sometimes, that's the first step to feeling more in control.

1. **Find a comfortable position:** Sit or lie down in a quiet space. Close your eyes or soften your gaze. Take a slow breath in and out.
2. **Begin at the top of your head:** Bring your attention to your scalp. Notice any sensation: warmth, tingling, pressure, or nothing.
3. **Move down slowly:** Scan through each part of your body: face, jaw, neck, shoulders, arms, hands, chest, stomach, hips, legs, feet. Pause for a few seconds at each part. Breathe into that area. If you notice tension, acknowledge it.
4. **Redirect when your mind wanders:** Gently return your focus to your breath and the next body part. No judgment. Wandering is part of the practice.
5. **Take time to reflect:** After scanning your whole body, take one final deep breath. Open your eyes slowly and notice how you feel.

When to use it? When emotions feel fuzzy or overwhelming, or feel disconnected or tense, and you need to ground yourself in the present moment.

IMPROVE the Moment

Even if you can't fix the problem, you can ease your emotional suffering. These strategies shift your mindset, soothe your nervous system, and help you stay grounded.

Imagery: Picture a peaceful scene or safe place. Use your imagination to calm your body.

Meaning: Find purpose in the pain. Even a small meaning helps.

Prayer: Turn to spiritual beliefs, core values, or Wise Mind for strength.

Relaxation: Ease tension with deep breathing, warm water, music, or stretching.

One Thing in the Moment: Focus on *just* this moment. Sip tea. Feel your feet. Be fully present.

Vacation (briefly!): Take a short break; watch something funny or sit in a new place. Have a plan to return after your break.

Encouragement: Tell yourself, "I've got this." "This won't last forever." Be your cheerleader.

When to use it? You're stuck in emotional pain and can't change the situation but need help riding it out without making things worse.

Radical Acceptance

We all struggle with acceptance, especially when reality feels unjust, unwanted, or out of control. Our minds try to bargain, avoid, or pretend. But as hard as it is to accept some things, refusing to accept them doesn't make them go away. It just keeps us stuck.

Your voice of resistance can show up as "This shouldn't be happening" or "It's not fair." That reaction is human, but it often creates a second layer of suffering because we're not just *feeling* pain; we're *fighting* the pain, too.

Radical Acceptance is the practice of ending that fight. It doesn't mean you like what's happening or approve of it. It means you're choosing to see the truth of this moment as it is. No judgment. No denial. Just an acknowledgment. In DBT, it's a core skill that makes room for healing. You don't have to agree with reality to accept it. But the more you practice Radical Acceptance, the less suffering you'll carry and the more strength you'll find.

SKILL 48

Practice Radical Acceptance

Radical Acceptance means fully opening up to the reality of this moment, even if it's painful. It's not approval or giving up. It's choosing to stop fighting what is, so you can start responding effectively. It says: "This is the reality I'm in. I will do my best to cope with it effectively."

1. **Name the issue you're struggling to accept:** First, try, "This should not have happened." Then say, "This is what is happening right now."
2. **Notice the urge to fight reality:** You may notice tension, clenching, or spiraling thoughts like, "Why me?" or "This isn't fair." Let yourself feel the resistance without judgment.
3. **Use present-focused language:** Say, "This is what's true in this moment." "I may not like it, but it is what's real."

   "I can't change this right now, but I can choose how I respond."

4. **Engage your body to support acceptance:** Try Willing Hands (page 105), Half-Smiling (page 104), or Wise Mind Breathing (page 20).
5. **Gently turn the mind toward acceptance (again):** When your mind fights reality, notice it—and gently return to the present. Say,

   "This is what's happening now. Resisting won't change it."

When to use it? When you're stuck in pain over something you cannot change, whether it has already happened, is happening now, or is beyond your control (like another person's choices, a diagnosis, or a loss).

SKILL 49

Turn the Mind

Turn the Mind is the skill that helps you recommit to Radical Acceptance over and over again. This acceptance is a choice, like coming to a fork in the road.

In fact, it's a choice you may have to make many times a day. Turning the Mind is when you notice resistance to reality and gently turn yourself back toward nonacceptance.

1. **Notice the fork in the road:** Ask yourself, "Am I fighting reality right now?" This could look like blaming, ruminating, saying things like, "This isn't fair!" or obsessing about how things should be.
2. **Pause and acknowledge the choice:** Tell yourself, "I have a choice right now: I can resist or accept." Face it so you can respond effectively.
3. **Turn the mind toward acceptance:** Gently shift your thinking. Try phrases such as:

   "I can't change this right now" and "Fighting this moment is adding to my pain."

4. **Repeat:** Every time your mind drifts back to resistance or judgment, notice it and turn the mind toward acceptance, again. And again. And again.

When to use it? When you catch yourself resisting reality or slipping back into old patterns of fighting what you cannot change.

SKILL 50

Embrace Willingness

Willingness means doing what works. It's about saying yes to the moment's reality and responding skillfully with the cards you've been dealt, even when you don't feel like it. Willingness is the opposite of willfulness, which is when we refuse to accept reality, reject help, or act out of stubbornness or pride. Willingness, on the other hand, is flexible. It's open. It says, "I may not like this, but I'll do what's needed."

1. **Notice willfulness:** Are you clenching your jaw? Refusing to act? Saying "Whatever, I don't care"? Pause. Say to yourself:

   "I'm feeling willful right now."

2. **Name the choice:** You're at a fork in the road: Willfulness leads to more suffering. Willingness opens the door to Wise Mind and effectiveness.
3. **Turn toward willingness:** Ask yourself, "What would it look like to be willing right now?" "What would help me move forward, even just a little?"
4. **Take one willing action:** It could be as small as unclenching your hands, softening your tone, or taking a deep breath and trying again.

When to use it? When you notice yourself resisting reality, digging in your heels, or refusing to do what's effective, even when it's what's needed.

SKILL 51

Half-Smiling

Lifting the corners of your mouth into a soft, relaxed smile—even if you don't feel like it—sends your brain a powerful signal that everything is okay. This isn't about faking happiness; it's about interrupting the feedback loop between a tense face and a stressed-out nervous system. You're smiling at your brain, not the room, letting it know you're safe, grounded, and capable of handling this.

1. **Pause and check in:** Notice your current emotional state. Are you tense, pissed off, or emotionally checked out?
2. **Relax your face:** Release the tension in your forehead and jaw and around your eyes. Feel your facial muscles soften.
3. **Gently lift the corners of your mouth:** Form a small, natural half smile. Think "neutral curiosity," not cheesy grin.
4. **Hold and breathe:** Let your breath flow naturally. Stay here for thirty to sixty seconds. If your mind wanders or your jaw tightens again, just reset.

When to use it? When you're feeling tense, irritated, resistant, or stuck in distress and want a gentle way to shift your internal state.

Willing Hands

This posture-based skill helps you shift from willfulness (resisting reality, clenching up, mentally shouting "NOPE!") to willingness (showing up and choosing to respond rather than react). It works by opening the body just enough to send a message to your brain, "I'm not fighting this anymore. I'm here. I'm open." This skill can be used discreetly in just about any location. You can rest your hands palms up under a desk, on your lap in a meeting, or while sitting on the couch during a hard conversation.

1. **Sit or stand comfortably:** Let your shoulders relax. Place your hands gently on your lap, or hang them loosely at your sides.
2. **Turn your palms up:** This is the key move. Keep your fingers relaxed, not rigid or forced. You're not reaching out or giving up, you're just opening to reality.
3. **Hold the posture:** Take slow breaths and notice what happens for one to two minutes. You don't have to feel willing to practice Willing Hands. Often, the posture comes first, and the emotional shift follows.

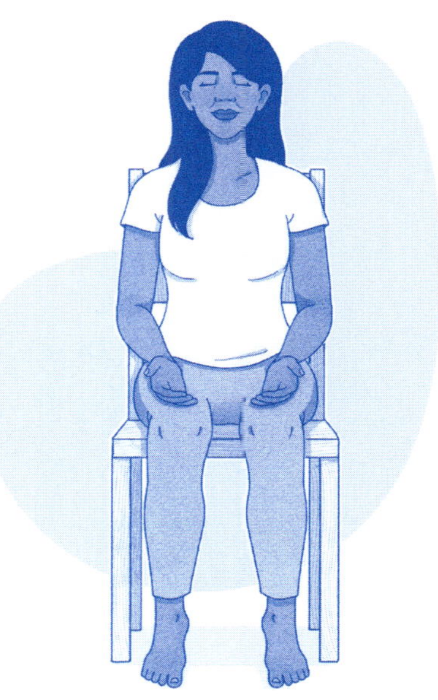

When to use it? If you're feeling defensive, closed off, angry, resistant, or like you're bracing against life. When you want to soften into Wise Mind, but don't know how to get there.

SKILL 53

Mindfulness of Current Thoughts

You are not your thoughts. When you observe them mindfully, without judgment, you build distance and clarity. This helps you choose how to respond instead of being run by every thought your brain throws your way.

1. **Get centered:** Sit comfortably, take a few grounding breaths, and bring your attention to the present moment.
2. **Observe your thoughts as they arise:** Let your thoughts come and go. Don't chase them, argue with them, or push them away. Imagine them like clouds going by or cars passing by on a road.
3. **Label the thought without judgment:** When a thought arises, silently name it. For example:

   "That's a worry." "That's a memory." "That's a judgment."

4. **Return to your anchor:** Each time you get pulled into a thought, gently return to your breath or body. No shame, redirect. See your thoughts as thoughts, not as facts or commands.

When to use it? When your mind is spinning with thoughts that feel overwhelming, distressing, or sticky, and you want to observe them instead of getting swept up by them.

Bonus Distress Tolerance Skills

These bonus skills are the ones I find myself teaching to clients again and again. Small but mighty, these tools help you get through moments of intense emotion, even when your brain is flooded and nothing else seems to work. Think of them as powerful reinforcements to your DBT practice. They are creative, real-life strategies that help you build resilience and get through without making things worse.

You'll find skills here like Alternative Rebellion, which channels that "I want to blow everything up" energy into something rebellious *and* effective. There's also Build Your Distress Tolerance Kit and On-the-Go Kit, which guide you in creating a personalized set of tools to turn to when emotions spike, whether at home or out in the world. You'll also get the Crisis Survival Flowchart, a visual road map I use in sessions to help clients figure out, in real time, what to do when they're overwhelmed and unsure which skill to reach for.

SKILL 54

Alternative Rebellion

Sometimes we feel the urge to say, "Screw this." That urge is valid. But rebellion that ends in shame or setbacks isn't real freedom. Rebellion doesn't have to be reckless. You can push back, stand out, or take control in ways that are creative, playful, and still aligned with the life you want to build. This exercise honors your need for autonomy or defiance without creating harm or regret, channeling your energy into actions that feel empowering and intentional.

1. **Notice the urge to rebel:** Ask yourself,

   "What rule do I feel like breaking right now?"

   "What am I pushing back against?"

2. **Name the need behind it:** Do you want freedom? Attention? Relief? Understanding the why helps you choose a better how.

3. **Choose an alternative rebellion:** Wear something wild. Say "no" to a should. Blast music. Take the long way home. Eat dessert first. Be silly on purpose. Express, don't destroy.

4. **Make it yours:** The best rebellion feels like you. Let it be a spark, not a wildfire.

When to use it? When you want to rebel without wrecking your goals, relationships, or self-respect.

SKILL 55

Build Your Distress Tolerance Kit

Think of this exercise as emotional first aid for a crisis like a panic attack, heartbreak, emotional numbness, or a rage spiral. It contains things that soothe you, ground you, or provide something to hold on to while a crisis passes. Use a small container or bag to keep your distress tolerance items organized. When emotions hit hard, your tool kit will be ready to go. Future you will be so grateful.

Check off those that you would like to put in your kit. Mix and match based on your preferences.

DISTRACTION TOOLS

- ☐ Puzzle book or adult coloring book
- ☐ Small game (e.g., deck of cards, pickup sticks, jacks, marbles)
- ☐ Word search or crossword
- ☐ Craft supplies
- ☐ Origami
- ☐ Sensory putty
- ☐ Fidget cube

SELF-SOOTHING TOOLS FOR THE SENSES

TOUCH

- ☐ Fuzzy socks
- ☐ Soft blanket square
- ☐ Textured fabric
- ☐ Stress ball
- ☐ Smooth stone

CONTINUED>

SIGHT

- Small photo album with calming or joyful images
- Affirmation cards or a "you got this" note from yourself

SMELL

- Lavender sachet
- Scented lotion
- Essential oil roller
- Herbal tea bag
- Flavored lip balm

TASTE

- Mints or gum
- Hard candy
- Favorite tea bag or single-serve coffee sachet

SOUND

- Noise-canceling earplugs
- Shaker egg
- Sound fidget
- A playlist of soothing songs or grounding sounds (on your phone)

GROUNDING AND MINDFULNESS TOOLS

- Summary cards of your favorite Mindfulness skills from Section 2 (page 17)
- Small item to hold while practicing Wise Mind Breathing (page 20)
- List of go-to grounding statements (like "This won't last forever.")

CARDS WITH COPING SKILLS AND REMINDERS

- Learn How to Cope Ahead (page 70)
- Pros and Cons of Crisis Urges (page 90)
- Affirmations or mantras (like "I've survived before. I can now.")
- Your top three DBT skills
- List of three people to text before acting on urges

TIPP PREPAREDNESS

- Instant cold pack (from a first aid kit, no freezer needed!)
- Cooling towel, gel mask, or ice roller
- Card with summary of TIPP with Paced Breathing (page 94)
- Reminder card: "You're in Emotion Mind. Use TIPP first."

CREATIVE TOOLS

- Notebook and pen for expressive writing or doodles
- Small pack of crayons or colored pencils
- Poetry or list of quotes that resonate with you
- Flashcards with "safe" journal prompts like: "What would Wise Mind say right now?" "What do I need to hear but can't say out loud?"

When to use it? Use it during a crisis but build it beforehand. This is a skill you create ahead of time to help you stay grounded and skillful when emotions run high.

SKILL 56

On-the-Go Distress Tolerance Kit

Emotional crises don't wait for you to be comfortable. Pack your emotional first aid kit like your keys or phone. Keep it ready, keep it close, and use it when it matters most. You can also include tools you can carry, store on your phone, or access from memory in a pinch.

PORTABLE TOOLS

- Instant cold pack (great for TIPP; easy to activate and discrete)
- Chewing gum, sour candy, or mints (for sensory engagement)
- A smooth stone, fidget toy, or textured fabric
- Small essential oil roller or scented hand sanitizer
- Card with pros/cons of crisis urges or a favorite DBT mantra
- Card with reminders of a value, goal, or something that matters to you

SMARTPHONE TOOLS

- Image folder of DBT skill cheat sheets and your My Crisis Plan on page 150
- A calming playlist (music, white noise, nature sounds)
- Favorite guided meditations or breathing apps
- An image folder of inspiring images, quotes, or affirmations
- Notes to self or texts from people who support you

MENTAL GO-TO SKILLS (NO OBJECTS NEEDED!)

- 5-4-3-2-1 Grounding (page 23)
- Breathe in for 4, out for 6 (TIPP with Paced Breathing, page 94)
- "This will pass" mantra
- Imagine your Safe Place (page 99) or do a quick Body Scan (page 98)
- Wise Mind ACCEPTS (page 96) or IMPROVE (page 99)

When to use it? When you're not at home or don't have your full kit with you but need to manage intense emotions in the moment.

SKILL 57

Crisis Survival Flowchart

You don't need to figure it all out in the middle of a meltdown. This flowchart gives you a way forward, one step at a time. Print it. Tape it to your wall. Save it on your phone. When emotions spike, let the process lead the way until you can lead yourself again.

> **When to use it?** When you're in high emotional distress and you need help figuring out which skill to use next.

CHECK YOUR DISTRESS LEVEL

Use the SUDS Scale (0–10) (see page 85)

- 0 = no distress
- 10 = worst emotional pain imaginable

If you're at a 6 or higher, you're likely in a crisis. Try any of the following to cope.

- **STOP to Create Space** (page 89)
- Pick a skill based on what you need. Use one or more of these categories:
  - **TIPP (regulate your nervous system):** Cold water, intense exercise, paced breathing, paired muscle relaxation
  - **Pros and Cons:** Weigh the urge: What happens if I act on it? What if I don't?
  - **Wise Mind ACCEPTS:** Activities, Contributing, Comparisons, Emotions, Pushing Away, Thoughts, Sensations
  - **IMPROVE the Moment:** Imagery, Meaning, Prayer, Relaxation, One Thing, Vacation, Encouragement
  - **Self-Soothe with Your Senses:** Use sight, touch, sound, smell, and taste to self-regulate
- **Ask: Is the Crisis Resolved?** Yes? Celebrate that you got through it skillfully! No? Try a different skill. Keep going. You're not stuck.

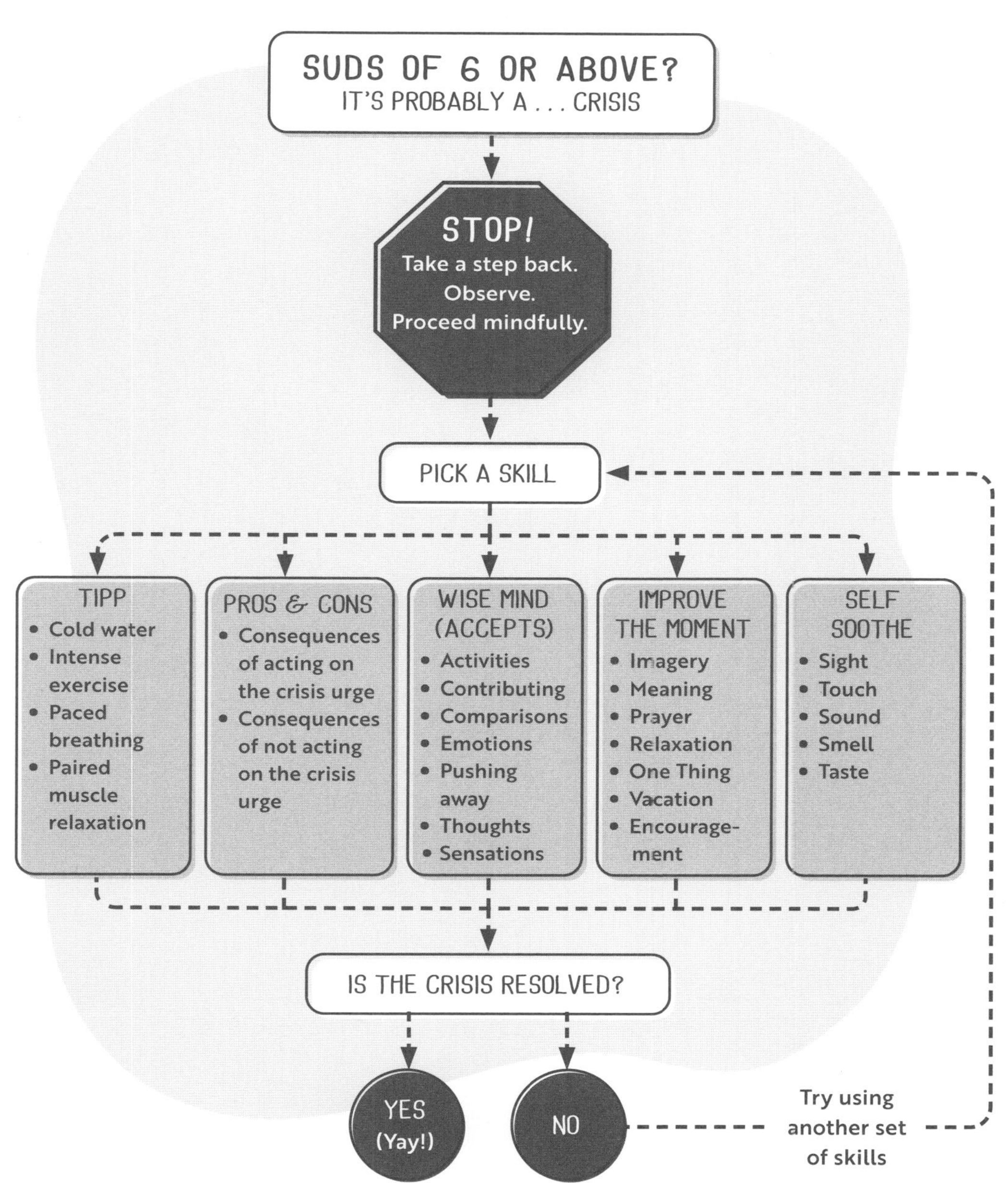
SUDS OF 6 OR ABOVE?
IT'S PROBABLY A . . . CRISIS
STOP!
Take a step back.
Observe.
Proceed mindfully.
PICK A SKILL
TIPP
• Cold water
• Intense exercise
• Paced breathing
• Paired muscle relaxation
PROS & CONS
• Consequences of acting on the crisis urge
• Consequences of not acting on the crisis urge
WISE MIND (ACCEPTS)
• Activities
• Contributing
• Comparisons
• Emotions
• Pushing away
• Thoughts
• Sensations
IMPROVE THE MOMENT
• Imagery
• Meaning
• Prayer
• Relaxation
• One Thing
• Vacation
• Encouragement
SELF SOOTHE
• Sight
• Touch
• Sound
• Smell
• Taste
IS THE CRISIS RESOLVED?
YES (Yay!)
NO
Try using another set of skills

DISTRESS TOLERANCE SKILLS TRACKER

Using distress tolerance skills regularly is a big part of coping with difficult situations and emotions and not making things worse. Use the following scale to rate the effectiveness of each skill on the day you tried it.

Rating:

1 = Didn't help tolerate distress at all.

2 = Helped tolerate distress a little so that I could cope for a while.

3 = Helped a lot; I tolerated distress and did not give in to crisis urges.

DISTRESS TOLERANCE SKILLS OF DBT	RATING				
Crisis Survival Skills					
STOP to Create Space					
Pros and Cons of Crisis Urges					
TIPP with Temperature					
TIPP with Intense Exercise					
TIPP with Paced Breathing					
TIPP with Paired Muscle Relaxation					
Wise Mind ACCEPTS					
Self-Soothe with Your Senses					
Body Scan Meditation					
IMPROVE the Moment					
Radical Acceptance					
Practice Radical Acceptance					
Turn the Mind					
Embrace Willingness					
Half-Smiling					
Willing Hands					
Mindfulness of Current Thoughts					

DISTRESS TOLERANCE SKILLS OF DBT	RATING				
Bonus Distress Tolerance Skills					
Alternative Rebellion					
Build Your Distress Tolerance Kit					
On-the-Go Distress Tolerance Kit					
Crisis Survival Flowchart					

SECTION 5

Skills for Better Relationships

Relationships can be wonderful, but they can also be confusing, frustrating, and sometimes downright painful. Perhaps you give too much and feel resentful, or you avoid conflict until everything explodes. Maybe you swing between people-pleasing and shutting down.

The Interpersonal Effectiveness skills in DBT help change that. These skills give you the confidence to speak up for what you need, say no when necessary, and handle tricky conversations without burning bridges or losing yourself. Whether you're trying to repair a relationship, build a new one, or let go of a harmful dynamic, these tools guide you in acting with intention.

Goals of Interpersonal Effectiveness

Think of this module as your relationship road map: fundamental strategies for being more effective with others *and* staying grounded in who you are:

- ✓ **Ask for what you need:** Use clear, effective language to express your needs, without guilt or aggression.
- ✓ **Strengthen relationships:** Build trust, handle conflict, and repair rifts while keeping the connection intact.
- ✓ **Respect yourself:** Stand up for your values and boundaries, even when it's uncomfortable.
- ✓ **Let go when needed:** Recognize when a relationship is harmful and walk away with clarity and self-respect.
- ✓ **Create new connections:** Practice skills that help you build meaningful, mutual relationships from the ground up.

INTERPERSONAL EFFECTIVENESS CHEAT SHEET

Skills for Better Relationships

GETTING WHAT YOU NEED, SKILLFULLY

- Clarify Your Priorities in Relationships
- DEAR MAN to Get What You Need
- GIVE to Improve and Maintain Relationships
- FAST to Maintain Self-Respect

BUILDING HEALTHY RELATIONSHIPS AND ENDING DESTRUCTIVE ONES

- Make New Friends
- Getting People to Like You
- Being Mindful of Others
- Ending Relationships

WALK THE MIDDLE PATH IN RELATIONSHIPS

- Balance Opposites in Relationships
- Validate Others to Help Them Feel Seen and Heard
- Recover from Invalidation
- Self-Validate to Honor Your Own Feelings
- Foster the Behaviors You Want
- Decrease or Stop Unwanted Behaviors

Bonus Interpersonal Effectiveness Skills

- Know When to Set a Limit
- Challenge Your Relationship Myths
- Use DEAR MAN When a Conversation Goes Wrong
- Joining a Group Conversation

Getting What You Need, Skillfully

Asking for what you want (or saying no to what you *don't* want) can feel awkward, intimidating, or even terrifying. Maybe you're afraid of seeming selfish, starting a conflict, or being rejected. Standing up for your needs doesn't make you a bad person. It makes you a skillful one.

This part of the DBT Interpersonal Effectiveness module is about getting clear on your goals in a conversation and learning to pursue them with respect and compassion for yourself and the other person. Whether you're asking for a raise, setting a boundary with a partner, or saying no to a friend's request, these skills help you communicate directly, calmly, and effectively.

In this section, you'll find skills to ask for what you want, maintain healthy relationships, and protect your self-respect. You'll also get guidance on how to decide upon your priorities in any given conversation. You have a right to your needs, limits, and voice. These skills will show you how to use that voice well and make it more likely you will get what you want.

SKILL 58

Clarify Your Priorities in Relationships

In any conversation, it helps to know your top priority. This could range from getting what you need, to protecting the relationship, to honoring your values and self-respect. Learning to clarify what matters most helps you communicate wisely and stay grounded under pressure. You don't have to get everything perfect. Choosing your focus before you speak makes your communication stronger, calmer, and more effective.

1. **Pause and ask:** What matters most to me right now? Getting my needs met? Strengthening the relationship? Protecting my self-respect?
2. **Choose your focus:** If getting your needs met is most important, lead with DEAR MAN (page 124). If protecting the relationship is most important, lead with GIVE (page 125). If protecting your self-respect is most important, lead with FAST (page 126).
3. **Blend as needed:** Real conversations often need a mix. You might use DEAR MAN to ask clearly, GIVE to stay kind, and FAST to stand by your values, all in the same conversation.

When to use it? Before asking for something, setting a boundary, saying no, or handling conflict (especially when you feel pulled in different directions or are not quite sure what you want).

SKILL 59

DEAR MAN to Get What You Need

DEAR MAN is a tool for expressing what you need while keeping the conversation respectful, confident, and focused. It helps you speak up clearly and effectively without aggression, defensiveness, or backing down.

Describe: State the facts clearly and calmly. Just the facts! ("I noticed...")

Express: Share your feelings and thoughts. ("I feel...")

Assert: Ask directly for what you need or want. ("I would like...")

Reinforce: Explain what's in it for them if they agree. ("It would help both of us because...")

Mindful: Stay focused on your goal. Don't get pulled off track.

Appear confident: Use a strong, steady voice and body language, even if you're nervous.

Negotiate: Be willing to compromise if needed. Offer options if it helps.

> **When to use it?** When you want to ask for something, say no, set a boundary, or assert yourself.

SKILL 60

GIVE to Improve and Maintain Relationships

This exercise helps you express your needs while remaining kind, respectful, and emotionally present. It's about protecting connection in your relationship. Even when emotions run high, you can use GIVE to stay steady, respectful, and effective. A benefit of being nice to people is that they are more likely to give us what we want. Kind, more compassionate treatment of others makes us feel better about ourselves.

(Be) Gentle: Use respectful tones and words. Avoid blame, threats, or sarcasm, even if you're upset.

(Act) Interested: Listen actively. Make eye contact, nod, and show you care about their perspective.

Validate: Acknowledge their feelings without necessarily agreeing. ("I can see this matters to you.")

(Use an) Easy Manner: Stay relaxed and approachable. A soft smile, gentle humor, or calm body language helps.

When to use it? When you want to maintain or strengthen a relationship, especially during a challenging conversation, or to reduce conflict. The question to answer for yourself is, "How do I want the other person to feel about me?"

SKILL 61

FAST to Maintain Self-Respect

FAST helps you protect your self-respect while communicating. It's about being honest, grounded, and kind, without guilt, apologies, or manipulation. You can speak your truth, stand up for yourself, and walk away with your boundaries, integrity, and values intact.

(Be) Fair: Be fair to yourself and others. Avoid judging or assuming the worst.

(No) Apologies: Don't over-apologize for your needs. Only say sorry if it's genuinely needed.

Stick to Your Values: Stay true to what matters to you, even if it's uncomfortable.

(Be) Truthful: Be honest and transparent. No lying, sugarcoating, or exaggerating to smooth things over.

When to use it? When you want to say no, set a boundary, or ask for something without doing things against your values or giving in, even if you worry that someone will be upset or disappointed.

Building Healthy Relationships and Ending Destructive Ones

Most of us want connection, support, and love. But building meaningful relationships doesn't always come easily, especially if you've been hurt before or never learned how to connect safely and skillfully.

This section focuses on two major goals: building and strengthening healthy relationships and recognizing and walking away from harmful ones. You'll learn how to connect with people who truly value you, show up authentically without chasing approval, and stay present with others in real time instead of checking out or spiraling into self-doubt.

We will explore how to find people who like you for who you are, engage in ways that build real connections, and remain mindful and emotionally present in your interactions. You'll also learn how to recognize when a relationship starts draining your energy, chipping away at your self-worth, or crossing your boundaries, and how to end it when necessary.

You deserve relationships that are mutual, meaningful, and emotionally safe. These skills can help you build those sorts of relationships and let go of the ones that aren't.

SKILL 62

Make New Friends

The processes of finding your people and building new relationships are aided by knowing where to look and how to show up. This skill focuses on two steps: finding close and similar people, and practicing simple ways to start a conversation with warmth and curiosity.

1. **Seek out people who live close to you and share similar interests:** You're more likely to connect with people who live nearby and share your interests or values. Some ideas to meet people:

   Join local groups or classes based on things you enjoy.

   Say yes to invitations, even if you feel nervous.

   Notice who feels safe, relaxed, and kind, not stressful or draining.

2. **Practice your conversation skills:** No need to dazzle, just be present and open.

   Start small: Smile and say, "Hi," or comment about the event.

   Ask open-ended questions, such as, "What do you usually like to do when you're not [at this event/with this group]?"

   Show genuine interest and share little pieces of information about yourself.

When to use it? When you want to make new friends and forge connections.

Getting People to Like You

Getting people to like you is about showing up with warmth, curiosity, and authenticity. Small actions, done consistently, build trust and connection over time. Remember, the right people will like you for who you already are.

1. **Show interest.** Ask about others' hobbies, experiences, or opinions. Genuine curiosity makes people feel cared for.
2. **Be warm and approachable.** Smile. Use open body language to invite connection.
3. **Share small pieces of yourself.** A hobby, a funny story, a small struggle. It is important to remember that a bit of vulnerability can create closeness.
4. **Use people's names.** It makes interactions more personal and memorable.
5. **Be dependable.** Follow through. Being reliable builds trust more than grand gestures.
6. **Respect boundaries.** You don't have to agree on everything. Connection grows from safety, not sameness.

When to use it? When meeting new people or building new connections, you want to be warm, genuine, and approachable while being true to yourself.

SKILL 64

Being Mindful of Others

Giving full attention to the person you're with—not just hearing their words but noticing emotions, body language, and energy—is a great gift. This skill strengthens relationships by making others feel seen, heard, and respected, and helps you stay grounded, even in emotional moments.

1. **Observe:** Notice tone, expressions, posture, and energy. Just watch and listen.
2. **Describe:** Silently label what you observe. ("She's smiling." "He looks upset.")
3. **Participate:** Fully join the interaction: nod, listen, respond without holding back.
4. **Use mindfulness:** Stay entirely focused. Gently pull your mind back if it wanders.
5. **Be nonjudgmental:** Drop labels like "dramatic" or "wrong." Just notice.
6. **Be effective:** Choose responses that support the relationship, not your impulse. Ask yourself: What will build connection right now?

When to use it? To deepen a connection, handle tough conversations skillfully, or stay present with someone instead of getting stuck in your head.

Ending Relationships

Ending a relationship is often harder than starting one. The following tips help you step away mindfully, safely, and with self-respect. Leaving a harmful relationship can be painful, but choosing safety, respect, and peace is a powerful act of self-respect.

1. **Check Wise Mind:** Balance emotion and logic with your internal wisdom and values. Are you acting from your deepest values? See page 18 for more about Wise Mind.
2. **Cope ahead:** Expect strong emotions like sadness, guilt, or fear. Plan and practice the skills you will use to manage in advance. The Learn How to Cope Ahead skill on page 70 is a good place to start.
3. **Problem-solve:** Consider how you'll communicate and stay safe. See page 62 for tips on problem-solving.
4. **Use Opposite Action:** Move forward with courage, even if fear tempts you to stay stuck. See page 60 to use Opposite Action.
5. **Communicate clearly:** Be kind, direct, and grounded. Say, "This relationship isn't healthy for me. I need to move on."
6. **Prioritize safety:** If there is any threat of violence or emotional abuse, your safety comes first. You do not need to explain or negotiate. Protect yourself and seek support if needed. Call the National Domestic Violence Hotline at 800-799-7233 or text START to 88788. Help is available. You deserve to be safe.

When to use it? When a relationship is unhealthy, harmful, or no longer aligns with your values, it's time to move on for your emotional or physical safety.

Walk the Middle Path in Relationships

In relationships and life, it's easy to get stuck in extreme thinking, believing you must accept or resist everything. You might feel like you have to be 100 percent right or 100 percent wrong. Healthy relationships require a balance of acceptance and change, self-respect and flexibility, validation and growth. These skills are essential for building strong, resilient relationships where you and the other person can grow, heal, and thrive.

You'll learn how to validate others and yourself, recover from invalidation, encourage healthy behaviors, and gently discourage ones that aren't working. The Middle Path reminds us that we don't have to choose between caring for others and caring for ourselves. We can do both.

Balance Opposites in Relationships

You can hold two seemingly opposite truths at the same time. In relationships, this may mean accepting someone as they are while also wanting change or accepting your own emotions while still choosing wise actions. Healthy relationships—including your relationship with yourself—grow when you balance acceptance and change. Instead of "either/or" thinking (such as, "I'm right and they're wrong"), try shifting to a more balanced "both/and" perspective.

1. **Reframe extremes:** Look for the both/and, such as, "I can forgive *and* set boundaries."
2. **Accept and encourage change:** Accept reality and work toward healthier dynamics.
3. **Validate and set limits:** Acknowledge emotions and maintain respectful boundaries.
4. **Notice extreme thinking:** When you hear yourself say "always," "never," or "nothing," pause and find a more balanced truth.

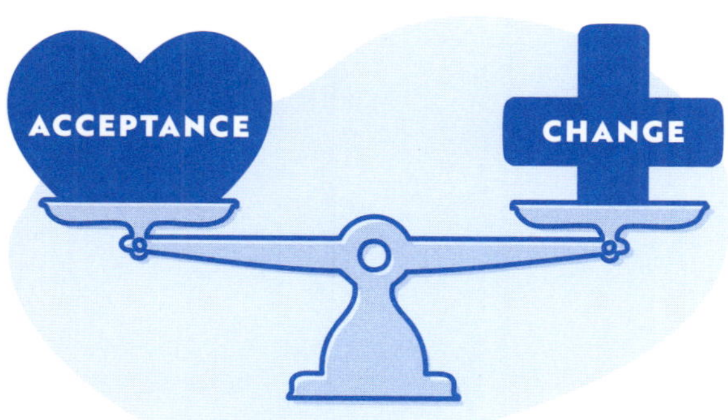

When to use it? If you find yourself feeling stuck between two extremes in a relationships: giving up or fighting harder, blaming yourself or blaming others, engaging in all-or-nothing or black-and-white thinking.

SKILL 67

Validate Others to Help Them Feel Seen and Heard

Validation means listening to someone with an accepting and open mind and showing that you understand their feelings, thoughts, or experiences—even if you don't agree with everything they say or do. It soothes emotional pain, builds trust, and makes conflict easier to navigate. You can also validate yourself (see page 136). Your own experiences deserve compassion.

1. **Observe with intention:** Pay attention to words, tone, and body language.
2. **Understand where their emotion comes from:** Ask yourself,

   "Given their situation, how does this feeling make sense?"

3. **Show understanding:** Use words, tone, and body language that convey empathy. For example,

   "That sounds really hard." "I get why you'd feel upset."

4. **Validate feelings, not behaviors:** It's okay to validate anger without validating hurtful actions. For example,

   "It's understandable that you're angry."

When to use it? To strengthen a relationship, soothe emotional tension, or help someone feel heard. This skill will help you build bridges where walls might otherwise grow.

SKILL 68

Recover from Invalidation

Being invalidated happens when your feelings or experiences are judged as wrong, unimportant, or "too much." Whether intentional or accidental, repeated invalidation can make you doubt yourself over time. Recovering from invalidation means staying grounded in your own truth, even when others don't see it. You can't always control whether others validate you, but you can always validate yourself.

1. **Pause and breathe:** Give yourself a moment before reacting. Strong emotions are normal.
2. **Name it:** Silently acknowledge: "I'm feeling invalidated. That makes sense."
3. **Self-validate:** Remind yourself:

   "My feelings are real."

   "It's okay to feel what I feel."

   "I know my truth."
4. **Choose your response:** Depending on the situation, you might:
5. **Calmly speak up:** Say, "I see this differently," or "I want to share how that felt to me."
6. **Shift the conversation:** If possible, redirect the conversation to a more productive or less triggering topic.
7. **Step away:** Take a break or walk away to protect your emotional space and regroup later.
8. **Let go of validation from others:** Not everyone will give it to you, and your emotional experience is still valid even when they don't.

When to use it? When someone dismisses, mocks, or minimizes your feelings, and you want to respond in a way that protects your emotional health.

SKILL 69

Self-Validate to Honor Your Own Feelings

Self-validation means recognizing and honoring your emotions, thoughts, and experiences without anyone else's approval. It's about acknowledging that your feelings make sense, that you have a right to your experience, even when others don't understand. Even in the best relationships, others won't always understand you perfectly. Learning to validate yourself builds resilience, self-respect, and emotional independence.

1. **Notice your feelings:** Pause and check in. What am I feeling? What story am I telling myself?
2. **Name it without judgment:** Say, "I'm feeling sad." "I'm feeling frustrated." Emotions are not wrong.
3. **Find the sense:** Connect your feelings to your experience. Such as,

   "Of course I'm anxious before a big change. Anyone would feel this way."
4. **Talk kindly to yourself:** Use gentle, supportive words. For example:

   "It's okay to feel this way. I'm doing the best I can."

When to use it? This skill is helpful when you feel misunderstood, criticized, or ashamed, and you can call upon it whenever you need to reconnect with your own emotional truth.

SKILL 70

Foster the Behaviors You Want

Behavior is shaped by consequences. When something feels rewarding, it's more likely to happen again. This applies to your habits and to encouraging good behavior in others.

The key is to notice when the good stuff happens and reinforce it in supportive, specific ways. Focusing on your strengths and others' helps build lasting, positive change.

1. **Notice and name it:** In yourself, "I made it to the gym today." In others, "Thanks for texting me when you were running late."
2. **Reinforce quickly:** Positive feedback works best when it's immediate. Praise, small rewards, and natural good feelings help behaviors stick.
3. **Be specific and genuine:** Instead of saying, "Good job," say,

   "I appreciate how patient you were just now."
4. **Stay consistent:** Change happens through repetition. Keep noticing and reinforcing small steps, not just big wins.

When to use it? When you want to build positive habits in yourself or encourage healthy, helpful behaviors in others.

SKILL 71

Decrease or Stop Unwanted Behaviors

Unwanted behaviors tend to decrease when they aren't rewarded or when clear, respectful consequences make repeating them less appealing. This skill involves being mindful of what you reinforce, what you ignore, and where you establish calm, healthy limits. Patience and positive reinforcement win in the long run.

1. **Notice the behavior:** Be specific. In yourself, "I want to stop procrastinating." In others, "I want to stop rewarding sarcasm."
2. **Remove rewards:** Ask yourself, "What might be reinforcing this?" Stop rewarding minor negative behaviors with attention. Set clear, respectful limits when boundaries are crossed.
3. **Reinforce positive alternatives:** Catch and reward small steps in the right direction.
4. **Stay calm and consistent:** Change takes time. Anger or harsh reactions can accidentally feed the cycle.

When to use it? When you want to reduce habits in yourself or discourage behaviors in others that are unhelpful or damaging to your relationships.

Bonus Interpersonal Effectiveness Skills

Sometimes, even after learning the core DBT relationship skills, real-life situations still feel tricky. You might wonder if it's okay to set a boundary, how to join a conversation, or if you're being oversensitive.

This section offers four additional skills to help you handle those messy, in-between moments. You'll learn how to decide wisely when to ask or say no, challenge old myths that can sabotage healthy relationships, join group conversations without fear, and recover skillfully when communication gets rocky.

These bonus tools are real-world, everyday skills that you can use. Remember, small shifts in how you show up can create significant changes over time. No relationship or social interaction is perfect. And you don't have to be, either. The more you practice these skills, the stronger your skills will become, and the stronger your connections will grow.

SKILL 72

Know When to Set a Limit

Some people say yes, even when they're overwhelmed. Others avoid asking for what they need because they fear seeming needy or causing conflict. And many of us struggle with both, especially in close relationships. This skill is for those moments when you're unsure whether to speak up and ask for support or set a boundary and say no. It helps you slow down and make a choice you can feel good about. Checking your values, goals, and timing gives you the best chance to act effectively.

STEP 1: CHECK THESE FACTORS

For each "yes," give yourself a point:

- Is your goal important?
- Does this fit your values?
- Is your relationship strong enough?
- Will it help your long-term goals?
- Is the other person likely to respond well?
- Have you given (or are you willing to give) what you're asking for?
- Are the facts on your side?
- Is the timing good?

Total points: ________

STEP 2: DECIDE WHAT TO DO NEXT

- **If your total score is 4–8:** Say no confidently.
- **If your total score is 0–3:** Consider waiting, softening, or choosing another moment.

When to use it? When you're not sure whether to make a request or say no and want to choose wisely based on goals and values.

SKILL 73

Challenge Your Relationship Myths

Sometimes, the biggest obstacle to healthy relationships isn't the other person; it's the stories we tell ourselves. These myths often stem from early experiences, trauma, fear, or culture. If we don't challenge them, they can sabotage even healthy connections. This skill helps you recognize the narratives you create and replace them with more effective truths. It frees you to ask for what you need, say no, set limits, and love with strength, not fear.

COMMON MYTHS AND HEALTHIER TRUTHS

MYTH: "If I ask for something, I'm selfish."

TRUTH: Asking for your needs is healthy. Relationships thrive on open communication.

MYTH: "If someone says no, they don't care."

TRUTH: People can love you and still have limits. Saying no isn't rejection.

MYTH: "If I set boundaries, I'll lose the relationship."

TRUTH: Strong relationships not only survive when boundaries are established but often grow stronger because of them.

MYTH: "I should meet all my own needs."

TRUTH: Healthy relationships involve giving and receiving support.

MYTH: "If a relationship is hard, it's wrong."

TRUTH: Challenges are normal. Conflict often signals growth, not failure.

When to use it? When unhelpful beliefs pop up and it becomes harder to set boundaries, ask for what you need to maintain healthy connections.

SKILL 74

Use DEAR MAN When a Conversation Goes Wrong

Even the best conversations can get messy. Someone might interrupt, attack, cry, or shift topics. Instead of abandoning your skills, you can reset using DEAR MAN: Refocus on your goal, stay mindful, and respond effectively. Skillfulness isn't about being perfect. It's about recovering when things go wrong.

You were introduced to DEAR MAN on page 124. Now try rehearsing the skill or using it when a conversation goes wrong.

1. **Notice the shift:** Are voices getting louder? Are you feeling overwhelmed? Is the topic drifting?
2. **Pause and breathe:** Take one slow breath. Give yourself space to respond wisely.
3. **Bring it back with DEAR MAN:** You can review this skill on page 124, or use this summary:

DESCRIBE: "I'd like to stay focused on [topic]."

EXPRESS: "I'm feeling overwhelmed and want to keep this clear."

ASSERT: "I need us to stick to one issue at a time."

REINFORCE: "That way we can solve this together."

4 **Stay on track with MAN:**

MINDFUL: Stick to your goal. Don't get pulled off track.

APPEAR CONFIDENT: Keep a steady tone and body language.

NEGOTIATE: Be open to finding a solution that works for both of you.

IF OVERWHELMED, TAKE A BREAK: It's okay to say: "I need a break. Let's pick this up when we're both calmer."

When to use it? When a conversation starts with good intentions but gets heated, tense, or confusing, and you want to remain skillful.

SKILL 75

Joining a Group Conversation

This skill helps you read the room, pick the right group, and enter confidently and respectfully. It's about noticing open moments and stepping in thoughtfully. Presence and curiosity open more doors than perfection.

1. **Look for an open group:** People standing loosely, glancing around, and taking natural pauses in conversation usually signal openness.
2. **Approach with curiosity:** Move closer slowly. Face the group with relaxed, open body language.
3. **Wait for a pause and join in:** When there's a lull, say something simple, such as,

   "Mind if I join you?" or "This sounds fun. Okay if I hop in?"

4. **Participate mindfully:** Listen attentively, ask small questions, and show genuine interest. You don't have to entertain; just being present is enough.
5. **If needed, move on:** If one group feels closed, it's okay to find another. It's not personal.

> **When to use it?** At a party, networking event, meeting, or any gathering where it would benefit you to join a group and get to know people.

INTERPERSONAL EFFECTIVENESS SKILLS TRACKER

Using Interpersonal Effectiveness skills regularly is a big part of getting what you need, improving your relationships, and maintaining your self-respect. After using each skill, use the following scale to rate its effectiveness.

Rating: 1 = Didn't help at all 2 = Helped a little 3 = Helped a lot

INTERPERSONAL EFFECTIVENESS SKILLS OF DBT	RATING				
Getting What You Need, Skillfully					
Clarify Your Priorities in Relationships					
DEAR MAN to Get What You Need					
GIVE to Improve and Maintain Relationships					
FAST to Maintain Self-Respect					
Building Healthy Relationships and Ending Destructive Ones					
Make New Friends					
Getting People to Like You					
Being Mindful of Others					
Ending Relationships					
Walk the Middle Path in Relationships					
Balance Opposites in Relationships					
Validate Others to Help Them Feel Seen and Heard					
Recover from Invalidation					
Self-Validate to Honor Your Own Feelings					
Foster the Behaviors You Want					
Decrease or Stop Unwanted Behaviors					
Bonus Interpersonal Effectiveness Skills					
Know When to Set a Limit					
Challenge Your Relationship Myths					
Use DEAR MAN When a Conversation Goes Wrong					
Joining a Group Conversation					

Support Tools

MAKE YOUR OWN DBT TOOL KIT

One of the best ways to set yourself up for success is to plan ahead, before you're in a tough situation. The idea is simple. Notice common patterns in your emotions, relationships, and habits, and match them to skills you can reach for when you need them most. This tool kit is a handy "cheat sheet" to see what skill to use when emotions run high. You don't have to get it perfect. Your tool kit is meant to grow and change with you.

HOW TO BUILD YOUR TOOL KIT

- **Notice everyday situations.** Those trigger stress, overwhelm, or emotional spirals. (Examples: fights with a partner, feeling invisible at work, getting triggered by social media.)
- **Match each situation to skills.** Remember to choose those that help you stay grounded and practical.
- **Write them down.** Having a clear list makes it easier to act when your brain feels flooded. See the following table for an example of what your list can look like.
- **Keep the list handy.** Keep a copy on the refrigerator, taped to the bathroom mirror, or saved on your phone.

The following chart is an example of how to organize a tool kit of skills. It features everyday situations that you find challenging and the skills that are most helpful in those moments. Be sure to continue adding to it as time goes by!

COMMON SITUATION	SKILLS THAT HELP
Feeling overwhelmed at work	• STOP to Create Space (page 89) • Problem-Solving (page 62), Self-Validate to Honor Your Own Feelings (page 136)
Arguing with my partner	• Wise Mind Check-In (page 18) • DEAR MAN (page 124) • GIVE (page 125)
Feeling shame after a mistake	• Self-Validate to Honor Your Own Feelings (page 136) • Opposite Action (page 60) for shame (hold your head high—you made a mistake, you are not a mistake)
Urge to impulsively text during anger	• STOP to Create Space (page 89) • TIPP (page 91), Self-Soothe (page 97) • Wise Mind ACCEPTS (page 96), Wise Mind Breathing (page 20)
Feeling triggered by social media	• Mindfulness of Current Thoughts (page 106) • Practice Radical Acceptance (page 101) • Opposite Action (page 60) (log off, shift focus)
Procrastinating on important tasks	• Wise Mind Check-In (page 18) • Opposite Action (page 60) • Avoid Avoiding (page 78)

CREATE A MINI-EMERGENCY KIT

Pick three must-use skills you can rely on anytime, anywhere. For example, you might choose the STOP skill, TIPP skills, and Self-Validation. Planning doesn't erase challenging moments, but it sure makes you ready for them. When emotions hit, your DBT Tool Kit will be prepared to go.

MY CRISIS PLAN

When emotions run high and you feel the urge to do something that may harm you somehow, it's easy to forget what helps. That's why creating a Crisis Plan ahead of time is so important. Do yourself a favor and leave a note to future you: a reminder of what works, who you can reach out to, and how you can stay safe. Take a few minutes to build your safety net today.

I know I'm in a crisis when I notice:

____

____

____

____

People I trust to reach out to for support during a crisis:

1. ____________________________
2. ____________________________
3. ____________________________

Good ways to distract myself and shift my focus:

Things that comfort, ground, or soothe me:

Ways to protect myself and create a safe space:

____

____

____

____

____

____

____

____

Other crisis survival resources I can use:

1. Crisis Text Line:
   text HOME to 741741
2. ______________________________
3. ______________________________

RESOURCES

If you ever need extra support, many resources are available to help you build skills, find therapy, and navigate challenging moments safely. You are never alone, and you don't have to face this work by yourself. The following resources can guide you in finding help, learning more about DBT, and strengthening the skills you've developed through this book.

CRISIS HOTLINES

988 Suicide & Crisis Lifeline

Call or text 988 for 24/7 confidential support for emotional distress, suicidal thoughts, or any mental health crisis.

Crisis Text Line

Text HOME to 741741 to connect with a trained crisis counselor anytime, for free and confidential support.

The Trevor Project

Call 1-866-488-7386 or text START to 678678 for 24/7 crisis support for LGBTQIA+ youth.

National Domestic Violence Hotline

Call 1-800-799-7233 or text START to 88788 for confidential help with safety planning and support.

APPS

DBT Coach

A full-featured app for learning, practicing, and tracking DBT skills. Offers reminders, skill explanations, diary cards, and coping tools. Available on iOS and Android.

DBT Diary Card & Skills Coach

Designed by a psychologist, this app offers digital diary cards, progress tracking, and a full DBT skills reference to support everyday practice.

FINDING A DBT THERAPIST

Psychology Today Therapist Directory

Search for therapists who may be trained in DBT and specialize in your unique needs. psychologytoday.com

DBT-LBC Certification Directory

Locate therapists formally certified in dialectical behavior therapy by the DBT-Linehan Board of Certification. dbt-lbc.org

WEBSITES

DBT Self Help

An informal online resource created by DBT users for DBT users. dbtselfhelp.com

DialecticalBehaviorTherapy.com

A user-friendly website offering DBT resources, skills explanations, worksheets, and articles for individuals, families, and professionals. Great for building DBT understanding and practice.

PODCASTS

DBT & Me

Two DBT therapists break down core skills with compassion, humor, and real-world examples.

A Therapist Takes Her Own Advice

A compassionate podcast where a therapist shares practical DBT and mindfulness tools while navigating her real-life challenges. Insightful, relatable, and skill focused.

REFERENCES

American Psychiatric Association. *Diagnostic and Statistical Manual of Mental Disorders* (5th ed.). American Psychiatric Publishing, 2013.

Behavioral Tech. "Core Evidence and Research Supporting DBT." Accessed April 25, 2025. behavioraltech.org/research/evidence/.

Behavioral Tech. "For What Conditions Is DBT Effective?" Accessed April 25, 2025. behavioraltech.org/research/evidence/forwhatconditions-is-dbt-effective-2/.

Bray, Suzette. *Borderline Personality Disorder Workbook: DBT Strategies and Exercises to Manage Symptoms and Improve Well-Being*. Rockridge Press, 2023.

Bray, Suzette. *DBT Explained: An Introduction to Essential Dialectical Behavior Therapy Concepts, Practices, and Skills*. Rockridge Press, 2022.

Harned, Melanie S., Kathryn E. Korslund, and Marsha M. Linehan. "A pilot randomized controlled trial of Dialectical Behavior Therapy with and without the Dialectical Behavior Therapy Prolonged Exposure protocol for suicidal and self-injuring women with borderline personality disorder and PTSD" *Behaviour Research and Therapy* 55 (2014): 7–17. doi.org/10.1016/j.brat.2014.01.008.

Jergensen, Kate. "Practice What You Preach: An Exploration of DBT Therapists' Personal Skill Utilization in Burnout Prevention." *Clinical Social Work Journal* 46, no. 5 (2018): 228–37. doi.org/10.1007/s10615-017-0633-6.

Linehan, Marsha M. *Cognitive-Behavioral Treatment of Borderline Personality Disorder*. Guilford Press, 1993.

Linehan, Marsha M. *DBT Skills Training Handouts and Worksheets* (2nd ed.). Guilford Press, 2015.

Linehan, Marsha M. *DBT Skills Training Manual* (2nd ed.). Guilford Press, 2015.

Malivoire, Bailee L. "Exploring DBT Skills Training as a Treatment Avenue for Generalized Anxiety Disorder." *Clinical Psychology: Science and Practice* 27, no. 2 (2020): e12314. doi.org/10.1111/cpsp.12339.

Stanley, Barbara, and Gregory K. Brown. "Safety Planning Intervention: A Brief Intervention to Mitigate Suicide Risk." *Cognitive and Behavioral Practice* 19, no. 2 (2012): 256–64. doi.org/10.1016/j.cbpra.2011.01.001.

Stiglmayr, Christian, Julia Stecher-Mohr, Till Wagner, Jeannette Meissner, Doreen Spretz, Christiane Steffens, et al. "Effectiveness of Dialectical Behavior Therapy in Routine Outpatient Care: The Berlin Borderline Study." *Borderline Personality Disorder and Emotion Dysregulation* 1, no. 1 (2014): 20. doi.org/10.1186/2051-6673-1-20.

Valentine, Sarah E., Sarah M. Bankoff, Renée M. Poulin, Esther B. Reidler, and David W. Pantalone. "The Use of Dialectical Behavior Therapy Skills Training as Stand-Alone Treatment: A Systematic Review of the Treatment Outcome Literature." *Journal of Clinical Psychology* 71, no. 1 (2014): 1–20. doi.org/10.1002/jclp.22114.

Winfrey, Oprah. "In Lady Gaga's Haus, All Are Welcome." *Elle*, November 6, 2019. elle.com/culture/music/a29683686/lady-gaga-haus-laboratories-elle-interview/.

INDEX

E

J

K

L

M

N

O

P

NOTES

NOTES

NOTES

NOTES

ACKNOWLEDGMENTS

Thank you to my son, Finn, whose heart, humor, and resilience inspire me every single day. To my brother, Tom, and my sister-in-law, Jamie, thank you for your endless encouragement, yummy meals, and laughter along the way. I'm deeply grateful to everyone who believed in this project and in the healing power of skills, connection, and hope. Finally, to every reader who picks up this book: Thank you for showing up for yourself. This work is for you.

ABOUT THE AUTHOR

Suzette Bray, LMFT, helps people regulate emotions, build stronger relationships, and navigate life's challenges skillfully and effectively. She's a licensed psychotherapist and the author of multiple mental health workbooks, including *DBT Explained* and *Borderline Personality Disorder Workbook*. Suzette spends her time writing, training clinicians, and working with clients in therapy. To connect or explore more of her work, visit SuzetteBray.com.

When she's not writing, training, or in session, she loves making art, building creative projects, and spending time with her son, Finn.